How To Books

Starting a
Business from Home

Starting a
Business
from Home

All the ideas and advice
you need to build
a profitable venture

GRAHAM JONES
4th edition

How To Books

Published by How To Books Ltd, 3 Newtec Place,
Magdalen Road, Oxford OX4 1RE, United Kingdom.
Tel: (01865) 793806. Fax: (01865) 248780.
email: info@howtobooks.co.uk
http://www.howtobooks.co.uk

Fourth edition 1999

British Library Cataloguing in Publication Data.
A catalogue record for this book is available from
the British Library.

Cover design by Shireen Nathoo Design
Cover image PhotoDisc

Produced for How To Books by Deer Park Productions
Typeset by Concept Communications Ltd, Crayford, Kent.
Printed and bound by Cromwell Press, Trowbridge, Wiltshire.

NOTE: The material contained in this book is set out in good
faith for general guidance and no liability can be accepted
for loss or expense incurred as a result of relying in particular
circumstances on statements made in the book. Laws and
regulations are complex and liable to change, and readers should
check the current position with the relevant authorities before
making personal arrangements.

Contents

List of Illustrations

Preface

A great deal has happened in the world of 'home business' since the first edition of this book was published ten years ago. Back then, in the late 1980s, we had just clambered out of a recession and many people were thinking of starting their own businesses. Many had been made redundant in the recession and were looking forward to selling their skills. Just ten years ago, this is how many home businesses began – they were a stop-gap and a useful way of earning a living, surviving redundancy. Now, though, home-based businesses are being taken much more seriously than ever before. No longer is a home business something you do until you 'find a proper job'! Indeed, many large corporations have seen the benefit of home-based working and have their staff based at home – the phenomenon of 'teleworking'. In addition, the rapid growth of the Internet has opened up a whole new raft of businesses that can easily be performed at home.

Because so much has happened in recent years, this book has been thoroughly revised. This is the fourth edition of what I hope is a practical guide to setting up your home-based business. It is a manual, rather than a book to be read from cover to cover. Even so, there is a logical progression from developing an idea and finding out whether or not you have the ability to run a business, to setting up your business, getting customers, keeping accounts, and expanding. Over three million people are now believed to run their own business from home, and the number is growing each day. As this book shows, the attractions of starting up your own business from home are enormous, but careful planning is required if you are to succeed. With the right start and good advice, however, you can succeed. And this book is designed to give you that start.

If you are short of business ideas, then start off with Chapter 1, which has a host of suggestions for a home-based business. If you know what you want to do, but want to find out whether or not you can do it, then start with Chapter 2. Advice on planning your business can be found in Chapter 3; the details of actually starting your business are dealt with in Chapters 4 and 5. People who have already started their own home-based businesses will find useful information on running them in Chapters that follow.

I would like to thank the following organisations for their help in the preparation of this book: Association of British Insurers; Barclays Bank PLC; Board of the Inland Revenue; British Telecommunications PLC; Data Protection Registrar; Department of Employment; HM Customs and Excise; Institute of Chartered Accountants; Lloyds Bank PLC; Midland Bank PLC; National Federation of the Self-Employed and Small Businesses Ltd; Rolex Watch Company Ltd. Special thanks are due to National Westminster Bank PLC for permission to reproduce the Cash Flow forecast form shown on pages 62/63.

I should point out that all characters referred to in this publication are fictitious, and any resemblance to real people is entirely coincidental. The terms 'he' and 'him' have been used throughout for convenience, and no sexism is implied or intended.

Trademarks mentioned in the publication are owned as follows: Filofax (Filofax PLC); Rolex (Rolex Watch Co. Ltd); Yellow Pages (British Telecommunications PLC).

Finally, readers of this book are cautioned to seek proper professional advice before making important business or financial decisions, and this book is not in any way to be considered a substitute for such advice. Readers are reminded that business law and regulations are liable to change so you should obtain appropriate, relevant advice.

In the meantime, though, good luck! Welcome to the wonderful world of working from home.

Graham Jones
gj@europe.com

1

Choosing the Right Business for You

CHOOSING YOUR BUSINESS

Virtually everyone dreams of working at home. You can start work when you like, do what you fancy, work the way you want to, and never have to worry about bossy superiors or office politics and gossip! From that angle, working from home is very attractive indeed. For most people, though, the thought of actually running a business from the front room is appalling. They like the attractions of working at home, but fear the responsibility and apparent lack of stability.

Even if you can overcome any worries about financial self-sufficiency there remains the single most important problem for anyone considering setting up their own home-based business — **What shall I do?**

If you want to start your own home-based business your first consideration must be to think very carefully indeed about the sort of work you might be able to perform, *and profit from*. To give you some idea of the sort of business you *could* run from home, here is a brief summary of the types of profitable endeavours you might want to start. The list of ideas is not exhaustive but should help point you in the right direction.

Selling a service

A business offering a **service** seems at first to be amongst the easiest to start from home. There is little equipment to buy, and you need relatively little space to work in. A telephone, a desk, and a typewriter are usually all you need to get going. Sadly, life is not so simple! Although service businesses such as writing, lecturing, designing and chauffeuring all seem to be prime candidates for home businesses, none are as simple as they appear. There is much more to writing, for example, than just inserting paper into a typewriter and then mailing the results to an eager publisher. Lecturing involves more than standing up in front of strangers and giving them the benefit of your knowledge. Service businesses like these may appear to be excellent options for the home-based earner, but they can be more difficult than some other home-based businesses, like craft work, or manufacturing. So consider them carefully, with all their implications, before deciding.

The following is a guide to the sort of services which are commonly the basis of home-run businesses; perhaps you will find that your hobby or interest has potential as a business.

WRITING SERVICES

Writing is one of the most popular forms of home-run businesses. However, despite popular opinion the vast majority of home-based writers are not happily producing best-selling novels. Such authors are rare. The bulk of home-based writing businesses provide written materials for a wide range of customers from greeting card publishers to producers of encyclopaedias. Most popular is writing for newspapers and magazines.

Writing for the media
Writing articles for newspapers, magazines, trade publications, radio and television is comparatively easy. Getting them published or broadcast is not. Do not expect to succeed immediately unless you have experience in these fields. Although some people *do* begin as **freelances** with no previous experience, most successful home-based writers have previously worked in journalism or publishing. If you want to run a home-based writing business specialising in article production for the media, and you haven't worked in publishing before, it is wise to gain experience in one of the other writing areas first. An excellent publication to help you find out more is *Writer's News*. This is published each month and every other month includes a bonus magazine, *Writing*. Details of both publications can be obtained from: Writers News Ltd., PO Box 4, Nairn IV12 4HU. Tel: (01607) 454441.

Writing for public relations
There are thousands of PR agencies in the UK, many of which are regionally based and support local industry. You will find local agencies in *Yellow Pages* listed under 'Public Relations Consultants', 'Publicity Consultants', 'Advertising Agencies' and 'Marketing and Advertising Consultants'. All of these agencies need writers. They need people to write press releases, to produce company literature such as brochures, and they also need people who can write or edit in-house magazines and staff newsletters.

Writing for local government
Like industry, local government often uses the services of home-based

writers for the production of leaflets, brochures and reports. One particular area of interest for home-based writers is in the production of tourist guides and leaflets. Local authorities also need leaflets on local history, interesting walks, shopping guides, and so on.

Writing books

Like writing articles, a home-based book-writing business is only likely to succeed if you are experienced in this field, or if you have a solid grounding in writing, gained perhaps from writing for PR agencies or local government. The average paperback book sells around 3,000 copies (hardbacks sell considerably less) and brings the author around 7.5-10 per cent of the cover price. Since paperbacks sell for a rough average of £8-£15 this means that each book an author writes could earn £4,500. To build up an annual *gross* income of £18,000 an author would need on average to write *four* books *every* year. Anyone interested in writing books should be sure to get a copy of *The Writers' and Artists' Yearbook*, which is published every year by A & C Black and is sold in most good bookshops. An excellent all-round guide is *How to Write for Publication* by Chriss McCallum, published by How To Books (4th edition 1998).

Other writing ideas
- editing company newsletters
- writing articles for foreign publications
- writing local guides for hotels
- writing course materials for educational establishments
- writing greeting cards
- writing short stories for local radio stations.

Other useful publications

Writers of all kinds will find publications like *Willings Press Guide* invaluable. This is not normally available from booksellers, but can be obtained by mail order. Contact Hollis Directories, 7 High Street, Teddington, Middlesex TW11 8EL. Tel: 020 8977 7711.

CONSULTANCY

Consultancy is a very popular way of running your own business, but consultancy in any field requires you to have a depth of knowledge and experience which your customers do not possess. It is no good setting up a home-based consultancy business if your customers know more than you! You will require a thorough knowledge of your chosen field, so setting up a consultancy service is best performed by people who have been employed in a particular speciality for some time. It could suit you if you are contemplating early retirement, for example.

Computer consultancy

Computer consultancy is a rapidly expanding area of home-based business. You should of course have wide experience of using computers, and you need to own, or rent, a number of different machines if you are to satisfy the varied needs of clients. Computer consultancy therefore requires a fairly large investment and a fairly large room for the equipment. You can of course specialise, providing expertise in the use of just one computer, one program, or the use of computers in a particular industrial setting; there are, for example, computer consultants who specialise in the use of computers in publishing.

Design consultancy

Design consultancy requires an artistic flair but you can specialise in virtually any field which takes your fancy. You can provide assistance in designing anything from a new living room for home owners on an estate, to designing the estate itself! Whether you choose interior design, industrial design, or any other kind of design consultancy you will need a portfolio of work to show your potential clients.

Employment consultancy

Employment consultancy can be virtually anything connected with the world of work. You can advise individuals on the jobs they are best suited to by using sophisticated psychological testing. Or you can simply act as an agent for local businesses, matching their vacancies with people who are seeking employment. Alternatively you can provide counselling services for the unemployed, helping them to improve their chances of employment. You could even set up a consultancy on how to benefit from self-employment!

Internet consultancy

With the rapid growth of the internet there are all sorts of consultancy services you can provide from home for this new technology. You might advise companies on how to set up their internet service or manage it within their organisation. Or you might be able to write and design pages for the world wide web. You could even advise the new internet companies how they can reach people who aren't on the internet! For more advice on the internet you could try another of my books: *Using the Internet*, published by How To Books.

Management consultancy

If you have managerial experience you can offer this service to companies requiring advice or information on management. Often management consultants will also offer marketing advice as well. Little investment is required for this sort of consultancy — you are literally selling yourself.

Planning consultancy

Every week local authorities up and down the country discuss millions of planning applications. These range from extending a lounge to building a motorway. Planning consultants help the applicants present their case in such a way as to increase the likelihood of acceptance. They also provide advice on changing applications if necessary. Planning consultancy is a very specialised home-based business so it is really only possible if you have, or are prepared to get, a thorough understanding of planning law. Further information can be obtained from the Royal Town Planning Institute, 26 Portland Place, London W1. Tel: 020 7636 9107.

Other consultancy ideas
- advertising consultancy
- beauty consultancy
- entertainment consultancy
- financial consultancy
- health and fitness consultancy
- marketing consultancy
- pet care consultancy
- public relations consultancy
- publishing consultancy
- relocation consultancy.

BUSINESS SERVICES

Every business requires **extra help** from outside sources from time to time. The sort of help required is easily provided by home-based businesses. Experience and knowledge are not always vital for these services but obviously they help. Accurate typing is usually necessary, but you can always learn that fairly quickly.

Book-keeping

Many small businesses cannot afford to employ a full-time book-keeper so they use the services of freelances. Many book-keepers work from home providing a range of businesses with basic accountancy help. You may also need to have a computer to provide computerised books for some businesses.

Mailing service

This kind of service covers a wide range, from simply stuffing envelopes with mailshot materials and posting them out, to compiling mailing lists. You can also act as a recipient for mail which companies want sorted and organised for them — this is often necessary when they are due to receive coupons from adverts, or competition entries, for example.

Telephone answering service

Many companies do not want telephone calls which interrupt their daily business. So you can offer to have your number placed on advertisements, or in promotions, so that you deal with the calls. You can also offer a telex service or a facsimile transmission and receipt service for companies who do not have the necessary equipment for themselves. (The cheapest way to do this is to buy a good computer and use the rapidly growing electronic network.)

Typing service

Every now and then businesses and industrial concerns have more typing than their full-time secretaries are able to cope with. Providing a typing service will help companies out of difficulties. An electric typewriter is necessary for this business, since very few firms will now accept the low standards of manual typewriters.

Other business services

- collection and delivery
- computer maintenance
- driving/chauffeuring
- filing service
- Internet support
- office planning service
- training services for employees.

HOME SERVICES

A number of services can be offered to **home owners**. Planning and design consultants have already been mentioned, but there are many other services which can be provided by home-run businesses for the benefit of householders.

Cleaning

With the growth in the number of working couples, there is less time for them to do the household chores. A profitable business can be made from cleaning local homes, and even local business premises. You do not even have to do the cleaning yourself; you can just administer the business and employ the services of other people to do the cleaning!

Catering

Many people nowadays require cooking help. They may need a birthday or wedding cake made or a dinner party organised. If you are able to cook, a home-based cookery business is possible. However, you will need a good-sized kitchen, plenty of utensils, and maybe even a van for deliveries. A simple home-based cookery business for other households can easily expand into a fully fledged catering business, providing buffets and dinners for wedding receptions and so on. You will need good contacts with local **catering suppliers**, and you will need to observe the current **health and hygiene** legislation when providing food to your customers. Check with the Environmental Health Officer at your local council for advice on how to set up a home cookery business. Not only are there regulations covering how you prepare the food, but also on how you transport it.

Decorating

This is a long-established home-based business. However, you will need lots of equipment, a van, and skill. You can avoid being considered a 'cowboy' operator by acceptance as a member of the British Decorators' Association. Tel: (01203) 353776.

Mail order agent

There are a number of mail order companies providing catalogues of goods which can be bought using simple credit terms. The agent gets commission on all the sales — around 10% of the purchase price. Some people make a reasonable profit from running a mail order agency because they attract a large number of local customers. There are also specialised mail order catalogues which run agencies, such as those for beauty products. Advertisements for the popular catalogue agencies can be found in most newspapers, and particularly in the *Radio Times* and *TV Times*.

Party selling

Like mail order agents party sellers earn a commission on the sales they make. However, it does require a little more work than running a mail order agency. You need to organise parties where customers can come and inspect the goods, and order what they want. You will need a car as you will have to organise parties over a fairly large area to avoid one locality becoming saturated with your attention. The range of goods you can sell at such parties is extremely wide and includes jewellery, clothing, food containers, cosmetics, even sex aids! To become a sales representative of the companies which use home-based workers you should contact them direct — many of them advertise in newspapers and in women's magazines.

Pet care

Many people will need their pets cared for whilst on holiday, or even during the day while they are out at work. You could offer this service and also a dog-walking service to people who cannot do this very necessary task for themselves, such as couples at work all day. If you know anything about grooming you can also offer to clean pets and trim their fur, etc. You could even expand the business and open up an 'animal hotel' for pets while their owners are on holiday.

Home laundry service

If couples do not have time to do the cleaning they will not have time to do the washing and ironing! A home laundry service is an ideal business to run from home — you can even reduce your electricity bill by performing the work in your customers' homes.

Other home services

- car valeting
- child-minding
- gardening
- hairdressing
- home tutoring
- house plant care service
- house sitting
- window cleaning.

CRAFTS

Many home-based businesses are centred upon the talents of an individual in a particular field. They operate a small manufacturing business by turning their hand to the production of goods which require the sort of individual attention not provided in mass production. Craft-based businesses also provide a number of items which cannot, as yet, be made by machines. If you have a talent for a particular **craft** then why not exploit it as your home-based business?

Carpentry

Wooden products of all sorts can be made in the home-based business, from carved ornaments to hand-made chairs — the choice is yours. You will need a good-sized workshop, tools, and plenty of storage space.

Jewellery

Hand-made jewellery is often highly priced and sought after. You will need talent, and specialist equipment. You should also be sure to have good security at home to protect any precious raw materials, like gems, silver, and gold. You should also make sure you follow the regulations concerning gold, silver, or platinum jewellery. Any jewellery you sell which contains these metals *must* be **hallmarked**. You will have to send the item of jewellery, prior to final polishing, to the Assay Office, together with the appropriate fee. Full details can be obtained from the Assay Office, PO Box 151, Birmingham B3 1SB.

Lampshade making

Hand-made lampshades can be designed to suit particular rooms, thus blending in with the rest of the decor. If you can manufacture lampshades you can provide interior designers and individual home owner with a valuable product. Local lighting shops will also be interested in hand-made lampshades. Like most other crafts, you can learn lampshade making at evening classes if you have no experience.

Sewing

If you are adept at sewing you can provide all sorts of products from curtains to clothing, including wedding dresses as well as a repair and alteration service. You will almost certainly need an electric sewing machine for this work, as well as a good relationship with a fabric supplier.

Toymaking

Hand-made toys are usually of the cuddly variety, although wooden or metal toys can be manufactured if you have the equipment and the ability. There are regulations which cover the manufacture of toys and these should be followed. You can get further information from the British Toy & Hobby Manufacturers Association, 80 Camberwell Road, London SE5 0EG. Tel: 020 7701 7127. You should also read the brochure, *Toy Safety Regulations 1995*, from The Stationery Office, obtainable from your local bookshop, listed in *Yellow Pages*, or by mail order from The Stationery Office. Tel: 020 7873 9090 or via the internet on www.tsonline.co.uk

Other craft ideas
- basket weaving
- candlemaking
- craft teaching
- dried flower arranging
- glassblowing
- ornament manufacture
- picture framing
- watch and clock repair
- wrought iron work.

Don't forget that you can always learn crafts at evening classes and at your local adult education centre. So if you do not have previous experience in any craft you can still learn enough to start up your own business if you find you have the talent. Once established, and if your work is good enough, you can join the Guild of Master Craftsmen, PO Box 28204, London N21 1WH. You should also subscribe to *The Craftsman* magazine. Contact The Craftsman Magazine, PO Box 5, Driffield, North Humberside YO25 8JD. The magazine is aimed specifically at people operating a craft-based business from home.

MISCELLANEOUS BUSINESSES

There are a number of home-based businesses which do not fall neatly into either of the two main categories of service or crafts. These businesses might contain a little of each type of category and include the following possibilities:

Board and lodging
If you have a spare room or two you can always earn extra money by taking in **lodgers**, or **holidaymakers** if you live in an appropriate area. Seek legal advice and get proper contracts drawn up so that there are no

difficulties over rent, liabilities, and so on. Draft contracts are readily available in stationery shops.

If you intend to open a guest-house you should register with your local tourist board. It can provide publicity for your premises. The tourist boards have also produced various booklets and leaflets on setting up guest-houses. Contact them at the following addresses: English Tourist Board, Thames Tower, Black's Road, London W6 9EL; Wales Tourist Board, Brunel House, 2 Fitzalen Street, Cardiff, CF2 1UY; Scottish Tourist Board, 23 Ravelston Terrace, Edinburgh EH4 3EU. People in other areas should contact the British Tourist Authority, Thames Tower, Black's Road, London W6 9EL.

Market gardening
With a sufficient large garden you could **grow produce for sale**, selling either from your home or a market stall. If you sell from home you should ensure that customers will not cause traffic problems by stopping at your gate. If you sell at a market stall then you will probably need a van. Useful advice can be obtained from the National Market Traders' Federation, Hampton House, Hawshaw Lane, Hoyland, Barnsley S74 0HA. If you intend selling eggs or any live produce, you must obey the regulations relating to their production and sale. The National Farmers' Union will be able to provide the most up-to-date information on the current regulations. The NFU is based at 164 Shaftesbury Avenue, London WC2H 8HL. Tel: 020 7331 7200.

Tuition
If you have specialist knowledge and communication skills you can **teach**. Many parents require extra tuition for their children, especially before important examinations. Other people want specialist education — they may want to learn to play the piano or to dance, or they may want to be taught how to type. Many localities have 'home tutoring' firms which advertise in local newspapers and these provide skilled teachers in specialist subjects. If there is no such agency in your area, you could start one, getting teachers to work for you.

Winemaking
Home-made **wine** can be very tasty and a real treat when properly produced. To sell home-made wine you need a government licence. This is not difficult to obtain, but you will also have to charge the appropriate duty on your sales and pay it to HM Customs and Excise. Details of the arrangements for this and for obtaining a licence are available from your local HM Customs and Excise office which is listed in the telephone

directory. The licence costs only a few pounds. You will also need a licence from the local magistrates' court to sell wine from your premises, allowing you to trade as an off-licence. Information can be obtained from the local Clerk of Justices — the telephone number is listed under 'Courts' in the telephone book. They will only charge a nominal fee.

Other miscellaneous businesses
- beekeeping
- car maintenance
- carpet fitting and cleaning
- floristry
- illustration
- photography
- portrait painting
- private detective.

The list of possibilities is almost endless and there are few trades or activities that could not be included!

DECIDING ON A BUSINESS

In trying to decide what kind of home-based business to set up there are three question to ask.

- Do I have a talent?
- Do I have specialist knowledge and experience?
- Do I have an interest in a particular activity?

If you have **talent,** then you should exploit it and earn money from it. You might not think that singers, actors, dancers, and comedians are running businesses. But they sell their talent and have to do the same business functions as other   home-based workers, such as book-keeping, dealing with the tax authorities, advertising their services, and contacting the bank manager! So if you have a talent which can be exploited, such as acting or singing, photography or painting, 'going professional' is a possible means of earning a living by working from home.

Many people start a home-based business using **specialist knowledge or experience**. As we have seen, consultancy is just one area of home work which depends on specialist background. Another area where expertise is required is in the provision of information. Many home-based businesses are run by people who work as researchers. They search out commercial or other information for their clients, who do not have the time or expertise to do the work themselves.

Do I have a talent?

Do you have any talents which can be exploited profitably? If you can answer 'yes' to any of the following questions, you need look no further to see what to base your business on.

If one of these questions has revealed that you have a talent for entertainment, or for some kind of artistic occupation, then you should consider exploiting it. After all, the pleasures of working from home will be more than doubled if you can earn money for something which you enjoy.

Check your talents

1. Can you write readable, interesting, factual or fiction material?

2. Can you take and process photographs of a high quality?

3. Can you sing, without fear, alone in front of a large audience, well enough to earn applause?

4. Can you make crowds of people laugh by telling them clean jokes you have invented yourself, and not feel self-conscious?

5. Can you dance in a number of different styles, to a high standard, in front of people without fear?

6. Do you design and make your own clothes, and are they generally admired?

7. Can you play snooker, darts or golf well, and win consistently in matches in front of crowds?

8. Do you act in amateur productions which are of a high standard, acclaimed by critics, and in which you have played a variety of well-received roles?

9. Can you play a musical instrument in front of an audience well enough to receive applause?

10. Can you interest local art galleries in your paintings or drawings?

11. Can you manufacture craft goods to a high standard?

But how do you find out if you are sufficiently talented to beat the competition? Your family will tend to say that your singing is marvellous, even if you are half a tone flat constantly. Your friends may claim that your snooker is better than Stephen Hendry's, even if you are really ranked one millionth in the world! So rule number one is:

● Don't let your friends and family fool you into believing that you have hidden talents.

Just because you enjoy amateur dramatics, or writing short stories, it does not mean that you will be able to make it as a professional. Anyone who exploits their talents competes in a tough and highly competitive world. Only if you are truly talented will you be able to survive. But, if you can't believe your family and friends, how can you decide whether or not your talents are worth selling?

The best way is to get some **independent assessment**. Go to auditions, enter talent contests, put your short story into a competition, try any way of getting an expert opinion on your talents. Perhaps the best method of testing your talent is in fact to try to sell it. Try writing an article for the local newspaper if you feel you can write, or try to get local hotels to take you on as a lounge pianist on a Saturday night if you think you could make it as a professional musician. This will help give you some idea of the extent of your talent, as will the reaction of audiences, readers or critics. Another way is to get criticism from professionals. Ask a writer to comment on your amateur work, or get a professional golfer to assess your game. Whatever your talent, professionals will be able to help you establish whether or not you should try to exploit it. So there you have your second rule:

● Get an independent assessment of your talents.

Do I have specialist knowledge or experience?

If you do not have any particular talents, or you discover that your talent is not of a sufficient calibre to exploit professionally, then you may be able to use your specialist knowledge and experience in your home-based business. Do you have any specialist knowledge? If you can answer 'yes' to any of the following questions you could have the basis for a home-based business.

1. Do you have any specialist qualifications?

2. Can you communicate effectively?

3. Do you know how to research information?

4. Can you offer solid opinions and advice based upon your experience?

5. Do you know facts and figures which other people in business do not?

If your answers to these questions reveal that you do have some specialist knowledge, then you could well use it in your business. But what are the key areas in which specialist knowledge is most likely to be required? The following are all areas in which people would like to buy services or products:

- advertising
- animal care
- business administration
- computing
- design
- health care
- home improvements
- information technology
- internet advice
- legal problems
- marketing
- public relations
- selling
- school examination subjects.

As you can see, the field is wide when it comes to selling particular specialist skills and knowledge. To find out if you have the necessary background and experience to run a home-based business in one of these, or any other subject area, try completing the following questionnaire.

1. What are your qualifications, from school, college or university?

2. What occupations have you had since leaving school?

3. What training courses have you attended?

4. What work experience courses have you attended?

5. What is your current position?

6. What is the main area of your daily work at the moment?

7. How many years' experience do you have in dealing with the kind of work in which you are now employed?

You should now have some written information to help you assess your suitability for work at home in a particular area. Let's look at an example.

Case study

Angela Petcare has two GCE A Levels, in Biology and Chemistry. She did not go to college, but went straight to work as an assistant in a veterinary surgery. She has not done any other job. She did attend a training course in veterinary work, which lasted for two weeks, and she also went to two residential courses, one on caring for dogs, and one on looking after small pets such as hamsters and rabbits. She is still working for the vet, making appointments, running the surgery reception desk, and looking after the animals under the supervision of the veterinary nurse and the vet. She has been doing this for the last three years.

What could we make of that? Angela's answers reveal that she has some experience of pet care, particularly looking after small animals. She has some scientific qualifications, as well as some veterinary training. Angela could perhaps consider setting up an 'hotel' for small pets. There are plenty of kennels to take dogs and cats for a short break whilst their owners are away, but very few places to take a hamster, a rabbit, a tortoise or a gerbil.

However, without putting down on paper her background and experience, this suggestion might not have appeared obvious to Angela. Answering this kind of questionnaire is therefore a worthwhile exercise.

Once you have assessed your specialist knowledge and experience and decided that you have something to offer, you need to decide what kind of business to set up. Will you simply offer your experience on a consultancy basis? Or will you actually manufacture a product? Write down your ideas, and then, in the same way as people who have a talent, get an independent assessment of the idea. You can ask your family and friends, but be wary, they may say that it is a good business idea even if it is not, just to avoid hurting your feelings. Get advice and criticism of your ideas from those people best able to criticise, such as colleagues, or people in a similar, though non-competitive, business.

Do I have an interest in a particular activity?

People who have never had a job and who lack the experience of an occupation should not give up hope. There are many home-businesses which can be started by unemployed people, based on their particular **interests**. Specialist knowledge can be gained from books, correspondence courses, and from training. In addition, there are other businesses such as window-cleaning, car-valeting services, chauffeuring, and so on, which do not necessarily require many years of experience to make them successful. So if you are unemployed, consider your own interests. A home-based business is possible without specialist knowledge and experience, though you will increase your chances of success if you are able to take some kind of training course.

CHECKLIST

- Try to find an activity in which you have a talent, some specialist knowledge or experience, or a particular interest.

- If you want to exploit a talent, get an independent, expert assessment of the extent of your talent.

- If you want to make use of your specialist knowledge, write down all your qualifications and experience to establish what you should concentrate on.

- Get an independent assessment of your business idea to see if others think it is a good one.

Some home business ideas

Writing services

Writing books
Writing for local
  government
Writing for the media
Writing for public
  relations agencies
Other writing ideas

Home service

Cookery
Decorating
Gardening
Home laundry service
Mail order agent
Party selling
Pet care
Other home services

Consultancy

Computer consultant
Design consultant
Employment consultant
Internet consultant
Management consultant
Planning consultant
Training consultant
Other consultancy ideas

Crafts

Carpentry
Jewellery
Knitting
Lampshade making
Sewing
Toymaking
Other craft ideas

Business services

Book-keeping service
Internet support
Mailing service
Telephone answering
  service
Typing service
Other business services

Miscellaneous businesses

Board and lodging
Floristry
Market gardening
Tuition
Winemaking
Other business ideas

Which of these could YOU do?

2

Can You Do It?

Having decided what type of business you want to start, you must now find out whether or not you will be able to carry out that idea and run a successful, profit-making business. This task requires complete honesty, and incisive analysis of your own personal skills. Without a clear and honest picture of **your own abilities** you could fool yourself into believing that you are business-minded when you are not!

In addition to assessing your own abilities you also need to check whether you have the **space, equipment, and legal right** to your business.

ANALYSING YOURSELF

The first step in determining whether or not you can run a business from home is to analyse your own strengths and weaknesses. Can you **cope** without direction? Can you handle the **loneliness** of self-employment? Are you **confident**? These are the questions which need to be addressed before you go any further. You might find that you do not have enough confidence to work alone, or could discover that you do not understand financial control sufficiently. Even if you continue with your plans, making such a discovery now would help you avoid problems later. Any faults or weaknesses revealed in this process of self-discovery can be corrected with effort and training. If, for example, you find that your organisational capabilities are poor you can take courses at local adult education centres, or by correspondence, which will help improve your ability, and make your business more likely to succeed.

Financial knowledge

Simply looking at your background and qualifications and matching them up with your ideas, as we did in Chapter 1, will not really determine whether or not you can run a home-based business. Look carefully at the answers to the questionnaire. Do they reveal any **administrative** experience or training? Do you have any qualifications in **financial** matters? Such areas are important in running a business. *Most businesses which fail do so because of a lack of control over finance, or* *because of faulty administration.* Analyse yourself accurately to be sure that you have the qualities required to keep a grip on finances and administration. Write down your answers to the following questionnaire to test your financial and administrative abilities.

Check your administrative abilities

1. Do you have any qualifications in mathematics?   _____

2. Do have any qualifications in finance?   _____

3. Do you have any qualifications in administration?   _____

4. What experience do you have of financial matters?   _____

5. What experience do you have of administration?   _____

6. What training courses have you attended
    on finance?   _____

7. What training courses have you attended
    on administration?   _____

8. Have you encountered any unexpected
    financial difficulties?   _____

9. Do you worry about personal finances?   _____

10. Do you run up debts? (If so, how
    often and how much?)   _____

11. Are all your personal documents, such as birth
    certificate, driving licence, insurance policies,
    etc, filed and easily located? (If not why not?)   _____

12. Is your usual work area in a muddle?
    Could you control this muddle?   _____

13. Is your personal life organised or haphazard?   _____

14. What do you understand about financial
    control and administration?   _____

Your answers to this questionnaire will show just how much knowledge and experience you have in relation to finances and administration — the cornerstones of any successful home-based business. If the replies show that your knowledge is slim, or even non-existent, don't think you are unsuitable for self-employment. Such skills can be learned. Your answers to the questionnaire will have revealed whether or not you need some kind of training for these important aspects of running a business. More details will be found in Chapter 5, but at this stage it is important that you know whether or not you have any weakness in this area.

The ideal candidate for a home-based business will have, among other things:

● qualifications and experience in financial and administrative affairs

● freedom from unexpected financial difficulties

● no worries over personal finances

● no major debts

● a well-organised home filing system

● a well-organised working and personal life

● an understanding of the need for financial control and tight administration.

Assessing your personal qualities

Even if you have discovered that your qualifications, experience and financial knowledge would be useful in running a business, self-employment requires a lot more than these qualities. You rely totally on your own abilities to provide income, and you must therefore be dedicated and able to work long hours — often longer hours than if you were employed to do the same job! You need to have **drive** and **ambition**, as well as confidence and a disciplined way of working. If you do not have such qualities your business is less likely to succeed. Use the following questionnaire to see for yourself whether or not you have those personal qualities which are vital if you are to make a success of your endeavours.

By answering this questionnaire honestly, you should have discovered a little more about yourself. You have been able to write down your thoughts about your ability to work long hours, the likelihood of you suffering from stress, and your flair for organising things for yourself and

Check Your Personal Qualities

1. Do you suffer from shyness? If so, under what circumstances do you feel shy?

2. Do you feel confident in most things you do, or are you often worried about the reaction of those around you?

3. Do you get tired easily, or can you work for long periods without difficulty?

4. Do you get on with people easily, or are you uncomfortable in the presence of strangers?

5. Do you like taking on responsibility, or do you prefer other people to organise you?

6. Are you trustworthy? Do people believe what you say?

7. Do you give up new projects easily, or do you always finish what you have started?

8. Can you work without direction from others?

9. Can you organise meetings efficiently?

10. Are you fit and healthy?

11. Do you have any disabilities or long-term illnesses?

12. If you have any medical problems do they hamper your current work?

13. Are you described by others as ambitious?

14. How ambitious are you?

15. Do you dream of running your own business?

16. Do you view the future positively?

17. Do you become irritable when there are problems?

18. What sort of difficulties in your working life put stress upon you?

19. Are there any problems at home which worry you? What are they?

Fig. 1. A personal qualities questionnaire.

directing your own working life. A self-employed home-based worker needs to be able to work confidently for long hours, without direction, and without suffering from stress and worries.

The ideal candidate for a home-based business will also have:

- confidence
- the ability to work for long periods without tiring
- the ability to get on easily with people
- the ability to organise and to work undirected
- stamina
- perseverance
- good health and fitness
- ambition
- positive thinking
- a stress-free personality.

Assessing family relationships

If your answers so far reveal that you do have the personality and ability to run a home-based business, do be sure that your plans will not cause **family conflict**. Many homes have been split because the problems of coping with self-employment had not been anticipated. It is better to air your views with your family and friends at the outset so that any difficulties can be examined and discussed. First clarify your own situation using the questionnaire on page 34.

Having answered this questionnaire discuss your plans with your family. Get them to answer the questionnaire as well, so that any problems you have not envisaged can be raised in discussion. It is better to air any problems before starting your business so that you can avoid them, rather than encountering difficulties in the future.

The ideal candidate for a home-based business will also have:

- an understanding and supportive partner
- an understanding and supportive family
- no major worries about home life
- no major concerns over children
- a healthy family.

In addition be sure that your family will rally round and help with the household chores which you will no longer have time for. If your partner is in a full-time job you will both have extra pressures to cope with home and family matters. Be aware from the outset that these problems will arise so that you will be able to cope. If you ignore the fact that a

Check Your Family Situation

1. Are you married?

2. Do you have a good relationship with your marital partner?

3. Do you keep secrets from your partner?

4. Do you have rows?

5. Does your partner work? If so, what does he/she do?

6. Do you have children? If so how many, what are their ages and at what stage is their education?

7. Do your children cause you problems and/or sleepless nights?

8. Do you have problems with your parents?

9. Do you have problems with your in-laws?

10. Does your partner know of and support your plans for running a home-based business? If there is no support, why not?

11. Do the rest of your family support your plans?

12. Do you foresee any relationship difficulties or problems at home which could arise because of your planned self-employment?

13. Do any members of your immediate family have major disabilities or illnesses which require constant attention?

14. Are household chores shared between you and your partner? Will any change be needed now that you are working at home?

15. How are your children cared for normally, and when they are sick?

16. What proportion of the household income will the business provide, according to your plans?

Fig. 2. Check your family situation.

home-based business will put pressure upon your home life you could reduce your marital bliss at the same time as lowering your profits. Be warned!

Assessing social relationships

By now, you should have got the general idea that starting a home-based business is about more than coming up with a useful idea and setting off into the land of millionaires! You need to consider every aspect of your life and analyse whether or not self-employment would fit into your way of life without causing too many problems. One area which can often be forgotten concerns dealings with other people. How will **friends** react? What will **neighbours** say? Neighbours may react strangely to your plans; working from home may reduce your social life and you may make more demands upon friends. The questions on page 36 will serve as a guide to the sorts of problems you will need to be armed against.

If you are determined to start a business from home you will want neighbours who are not going to complain and who do not really mind you working from the spare room. If neighbours do complain and worry about the effect of your work on the value of their house it can make life a misery, and reduce your effectiveness in business, thus reducing profits. So it is wise to advise your neighbours of your plans in the first place, and seek ways of coming to a compromise over any disagreements. If your friends meet your neighbours socially it is wise to get on good terms with neighbours from the outset because any problems could ripple through an entire network of friends!

With careful planning, this situation should not arise. However, working from home is a lonely occupation, and you may make demands on friends for extra social outings, just so that you can get outside the house! Look at your circle of friends and assess the likelihood of them accepting this increased social activity. Tell your friends of this possibility, and check their reaction! Your business life will be boosted by a good social life, so it is wise to consider now the problems which may arise in the future.

The ideal candidate for a home-based business will have:

● understanding neighbours

● a good relationship with neighbours

● good friends who can be relied upon.

Check Your Social Relationships

1. How well do you get on with your neighbours?
2. Have you mentioned your plans to your neighbours? If so, what was their initial reaction?
3. Are your neighbours the sort of people who complain readily?
4. Are your neighbours particularly keen on keeping property values as high as possible?
5. Do you have good friends? Can they be called upon as shoulders to cry on?
6. Do your friends enjoy socialising, or are they stay-at-home people?
7. Do your friends and neighbours mix socially?
8. Have you told your friends of your proposed home-based business? What was their reaction?

Fig. 3. Social relationships questionnaire.

ANALYSING YOUR HOME ENVIRONMENT

Your home is going to be your business base, so it is important that it should provide the facilities you need for the business you intend to start. For example, if you intend running a furniture-making business you might find difficulty operating from a twentieth-floor studio flat, although a writer could happily work in such environment. You must analyse all the features of your home which could be an advantage and those which could hamper your work. Start by answering the following questionnaire so that you have the basic facts about your home in front of you.

This information will enable you to check that your home will provide the basic requirements for your work. For example, working at home will almost certainly require **central heating**. You will not be able to work effectively in winter if your home is cold all day. Ideally you should be able to use a **spare room** for your business activities so that work does not intrude on home life. Also, a **self-contained** environment

Check Your Home Environment

1. What type of home is it (House, Flat, Bungalow, Caravan, etc)?

2. How many rooms does it have?

3. How old is it?

4. What material is it built with?

5. Is your home self-contained, or part of a block?

6. How many outbuildings (shed, garage, etc) are there?

7. How many spare rooms are there?

8. What facilities are there (eg hot water, gas, electricity, central heating, etc)?

Fig. 4. Home environment questionnaire.

is better if your work is likely to be noisy. Of course, you do not necessarily have to move house in order to have the perfect workplace, but bear in mind that if your home is not ideal for your kind of business there may be problems in the future. The best arrangement would be:

● a solidly constructed building that is warm in winter
● a spare room
● a home which is self-contained and not part of a block.

But if you cannot achieve this ideal, do not give up. You may still be able to work from home in a tower block, providing it does not upset the neighbours, and assuming that you will not have to haul tons of equipment up and down the stairs! Just think carefully about your circumstances.

If you do not have a spare room, think of the ways around the problem. Could you convert the garage, for example, or could the garden shed be used? Is the loft large enough to be converted into a spare room? Think of all these alternatives and work out the costs of making any conversions. Discuss other possibilities with your family, such as using half of the dining room for your office. If your only problem is a lack of storage space for raw materials, why not all have a spring clean one weekend, throwing out as much rubbish as possible, and selling off any unwanted items? Perhaps you can release extra cupboard space which could solve your problem.

Space required

To determine the amount of space you need list the equipment and furniture required in your work. The following questions will help:

1. What basic equipment do you require (eg desk, filing cabinet, chair, table, etc)?

2. Do you need any specialist equipment?

3. What services do you need (eg electricity, gas, water, phone)?

This questionnaire will highlight the amount of space needed. Two desks, a sink with running water and four filing cabinets will obviously need more space than just a table and a chair. However, a good rule of thumb is to look at your initial requirements for space and then double it. You will be amazed how quickly you accumulate material, so it's better to have space available at the outset than to become cramped and find it difficult to work.

Whatever type of business you are intending to start, you will almost certainly need to allow space for the following items:

*   desk
*   chair
*   four-drawer filing cabinet
*   bookcase
*   large cupboard.

Legal considerations

Contrary to popular belief, an Englishman's home is not his castle! There is a long list of laws and regulations which control what we can and cannot do in our own homes. The main legal area to be investigated before starting up is whether or not you are legally entitled to use your home for business purposes. There are many laws which prevent people running profit-making enterprises in their homes. It is wise to check your own position before you begin, otherwise you may end up in trouble once you have started your business!

Checking for planning permission

The first area to consider is **planning permission**. The planning legislation basically divides properties into those which can be used for **commercial purposes**, and those which are purely **domestic**. Planning authorities are obliged to prevent residential areas being infiltrated by offices and factories, and so legislation ensures that a house which has been used for domestic purposes cannot be used for commercial gain without planning permission. In most cases such permission will not be given, simply because the local authority's aim is to keep areas of housing and business as separate as possible.

If you intend using your home for business purposes you could fall foul of this area of legislation. Without planning permission, the authorities could obtain a court injunction restraining you from carrying out your business from home. However, it is still possible to work from home without contravening the planning legislation. The Government has relaxed the rules somewhat, since it is encouraging more and more people to start small businesses. Consequently planning permission is not needed if your business will not 'materially change the use' of any part of your home, but this definition is open to interpretation, and various local authorities construe it differently.

Generally, you will not need planning permission if you do not alter the structure of your home, and if the rooms you use for your business are still largely available for ordinary domestic functions. If you use a spare bedroom as an office but can still use it as a guest room as well you will not have 'materially changed' the use of the room, so planning permission would not be required. However, check with the local planning authority before starting work. Each area of the country is different, and there may also be local by-laws applying which affect the use of your premises for business purposes. If you have any doubts, then contact a **planning consultant**. You can obtain the names of the ones in your area from your local council, or contact the Royal Town Planning Institute, 26 Portland Place, London W1N 4BE. Tel: 020 7636 9107.

If you do need planning permission, you will have to get a **change of use certificate**. These are difficult to obtain in residential areas and you may well find it easier to abandon your ideas for a home-based business and look for business premises.

Landlords

If you rent your home your landlord may object to you using his building as a base for your business. If you don't check this out, and start your business regardless, you may ultimately find yourself **evicted** for being in breach of your contract with your landlord. Council tenants must also check with their local authority that they will not break any rules by working at home.

Property deeds

If you own your own home the **deeds** of the house may contain paragraphs relating to its possible business use. Often when large estates are built the developers include covenants or clauses in the deeds forbidding the use of the dwellings for any kind of business purpose. This is to help ensure that the area remains primarily residential. If this is so in your case, obtain legal advice on whether or not to proceed.

You may find that running a business from home against the written word of the property deeds is not a problem unless your neighbours complain. They might then be able to obtain an injunction against you to stop working in contravention of the property deeds. Few neighbours would take this step if your business was not troublesome or causing problems in the area. However, if you plan to operate a noisy motorcycle manufacturing plant in the garage, you could end up in trouble! Whatever you plan to do from home get a solicitor to check your property deeds so that you know of any risks you may be taking.

Mortgage restrictions

Virtually every **mortgage** agreement contains a clause relating to the business use of the premises. Mortgage companies will not lend you money to buy a house if you then use it as a base for commercial gain. They, like planning authorities, clearly distinguish between residential and business properties and argue that if you want to run a business from a house you require a commercial property loan and not a domestic mortgage.

Fortunately, most mortgage companies are prepared to bend the rules slightly providing you can establish that you are not changing the basic use of the premises. If your home is still to be used mainly for residential purposes, the mortgage company is likely to continue your mortgage on the existing basis. However, if you plan to convert all of the bedrooms into a mini-factory, the company is unlikely to turn a blind eye! Check your mortgage documents to find out whether or not you are going to breach any clauses of the contract. If the contract does forbid the business use of the premises get advice from your solicitor as to how to proceed. However, the fact that an estimated two million people already work from their own home, is testimony to the flexibility that exists.

Insurance cover

Working from home will almost certainly affect type of policy which covers your house, and now might be a good time to inform your insurance company. Find out what sort of deal they offer, but don't commit yourself to their policy simply because you've used them before — it pays to shop around first! For more details on insurance see page 146.

ANALYSING THE COMPETITION

Once you have analysed yourself, your home and your legal situation you have one final item to consider — the possible **competition**. Competition can be healthy, but it can also destroy a business. Find out who your competitors are and how they might affect your proposals.

First write down a few basic facts about your proposed business. Use the following questions to help you focus your attention.

1. Will you be operating a purely local service, or will you be conducting your business on a national basis?

2. Will you be offering added extras which no other competitor can provide?

If you intend operating on a purely local basis arm yourself with the following publications:

● *Yellow Pages*
● a local directory
● local newspapers.

If you are operating on a national basis you will need the following publications:

● *Kelly's Commercial Directory* (www.kellys.co.uk)
● national newspapers/magazines
● any specialist directories/trade publications relating to your proposed business.

Whether operating locally or nationally:

● Scour these publications for advertisers and list of people who provide similar services to you.

Assessing the competition	Name of competitor	Name of another competitor					
Good range of products/services							
Quality of products/services							
Value for money							
Well-known brand names							
Branches/outlets							
Amount of advertising							
Quality of advertising							
Quality of customer service							
General image and reputation							
Creative and innovative							
Local presence							
TOTAL SCORE							

Fig. 5. Assessing the competition.

● Telephone those firms most likely to compete and ask for information about their company, products and services (you can pose as a potential customer).
● Ask for any brochures they produce, and read them carefully.

The information you collect in this way will either make you change your basic plans about your proposed business because the competition is too strong, or support your ideas because the competition is unable to provide the sort of service you can offer. Your local public reference library will be a mine of information. You should also be sure to cut out and keep the advertisements and promotional material given out by any competitors. In this way you will be able to build up a profile of your competitors and assess whether or not your proposals would be squashed at birth!

Assessing the competition

Rate each competitor 1 to 10 in each column of the chart on page 42. Use the scores to identify your main competitors and any aspects where you expect to do better.

CHECKLIST

In deciding whether you can start your own business at home, you need to assess

● your financial and administrative ability
● your personal attributes and suitability to working on your own at home
● your relationships with your family, friends and neighbours, and their attitude to your plans
● the suitability of your home for the work you propose to do
● any legal problems
● the competition and its effects on your plans.

3

Your Business Plan

WHY HAVE A BUSINESS PLAN?

So far you've written a great deal about your ideas and about you as a person. Now it's time to put all this information together into one, comprehensive document — **the business plan**.

The business plan will have at least two functions:

- It will help clarify exactly what you intend to achieve with your business.
- It will show potential investors that you have thoroughly researched and prepared everything for starting a business — that you have a serious proposal worth consideration.

PLANNING THE CONTENTS

Your business plan should be a concise, easy-to-understand guide and reference to everything concerning your proposed business. It will probably be several dozen pages long, and contain at least the following information:

- basic data on you and your background
- an introduction to why your business will be sought after
- a list of skills required for the proposed business
- the premises and facilities available for the business
- your current financial status, income, expenditure and assets
- expected start-up costs (eg purchase of equipment)
- details of who your customers will be, and how many
- information on how you propose to attract and keep them
- the expected income in each of the first three years
- the likely need for outside cash injections
- a cash flow forecast for each of the first three years
- a list of the risks the business may face
- a statement of how you expect your business to be situated in three years' time.

Your business plan therefore needs to be very well researched and clearly thought out. It will provide specific information on how successful you are likely to be, and will provide your professional advisers, such as your bank manager, with much necessary data. Of course, business plans are not meant to be the final word. You will need to update your plan each year at least as customers come and go, and projected income and expenditure changes. A business plan must be a flexible document, but it must be as accurate as you can possibly make it. So let's start producing *your* business plan. You will need:

- your written business ideas produced in Chapter 1
- all the personal data produced in Chapter 2
- the information on competitors produced in Chapter 2
- the information on your home produced in Chapter 2
- all documents relating to your current financial status including bank statements, building society books, mortgage documents, insurance policies, and so on
- a calculator
- cash flow forms like the one shown on pages 62-63.

You will also need a clear mind, plenty of time, and no distractions. The plan you are about to write is the foundation of your proposed enterprise. Any cracks or faults could cause the business to collapse so be sure in your own mind that your business plan is as accurate, realistic and objective as possible.

PUTTING THE PIECES TOGETHER

To start off, use the information gathered on yourself in Chapters 1 and 2 to write an introduction about yourself, your background and your experience. Then, using the ideas produced after reading Chapter 1, write a detailed description of the type of business you propose to run. The next task is to write a few paragraphs stating very clearly why you decided to start up your own business, why you think you will succeed, and what your enterprise will provide which cannot be obtained from other organisations. This section should also contain something on the kind of skills required in your proposed business, and how you intend to gain those skills if you do not already possess them.

The remainder of this introductory section will give information on the premises you have and the facilities and services which are available. If you will need additional facilities you must indicate how much they

- ☐ accounting books
  (see Chapter 5)
- ☐ book to note down supplies
  needed
- ☐ book to note down orders
- ☐ bookends
- ☐ book shelves
- ☐ box files
- ☐ calculator
- ☐ car/van
- ☐ card filing system, including
  blank cards
- ☐ cash box
- ☐ chair
- ☐ clear A4 pockets for filing
- ☐ computer and printer
- ☐ date stamp
- ☐ desk
- ☐ desk lamp
- ☐ diary
- ☐ elastic bands
- ☐ electric typewriter/word
  processor
- ☐ electrical adaptors/multi-
  sockets
- ☐ envelopes
- ☐ fax machine
- ☐ four-drawer filing cabinets
- ☐ headed notepaper/
  compliment slips/
  business cards
- ☐ heater if there is no central
  heating
- ☐ hole punch
- ☐ in trays
- ☐ internet access
- ☐ kettle, coffee cups, etc, if
  there is no access to a
  kitchen
- ☐ letter opener, scissors
- ☐ mobile phone
- ☐ notebooks
- ☐ paper (bond and bank for
  top sheets and copies)
- ☐ paperclips
- ☐ pencils
- ☐ pens and refills
- ☐ photocopier and
- ☐ photocopying paper
- ☐ postage scales
- ☐ postage stamps
- ☐ reference books including
  a good dictionary, extra
  telephone directories, an
  encyclopaedia, bus and
  rail timetables, and any
  books or directories
  specific to your proposed
  business
- ☐ ring binders
- ☐ ruler
- ☐ scissors
- ☐ signs for van
- ☐ specialist software
- ☐ stamping pad and ink
- ☐ stamps for 'First Class',
  'Urgent', 'Paid'
- ☐ staple remover
- ☐ stapler
- ☐ sticky tape/glue
- ☐ string
- ☐ suspension files for filing
- ☐ telephone
- ☐ telephone answering
  machine
- ☐ wall calendar

Fig. 6. A checklist of start-up costs.

will cost and where you propose getting the money. Once you have done this you will have finished the basic introduction, and you will be able to move on to the more complex task of predicting finances.

Writing the financial information

Following the basic introduction you will need to provide an over-view of your current financial situation, and the costs which are likely to be incurred in setting up your proposed business. This section needs to be as accurate as possible, and if anything it is better to overestimate the costs slightly. Many businesses fail in the first year of operation because their owners underestimate the initial costs.

In writing this section of the report the first thing to do is to set out your current financial status, showing:

1. **Assets** — these could be divided into current assets (which could be immediately turned into cash if necessary, such as cash in hand or money in bank accounts), and fixed assets (such as the business property).

2. **Liabilities** — again, these could be divided into current and fixed liabilities.

3. Other relevant financial data — including any insurance policies due to mature and pensions held.

Calculating start-up costs

Having listed this data you will then need to estimate your *start-up costs*. Think very carefully before you come to a final figure. Golden rule:

● **Do not underestimate your start-up costs**.

To calculate these costs list all the items you need to run your business efficiently. Then get accurate costings of the items you list by visiting the shops, by getting written quotations from suppliers of items like stationery. *Do not try to guess the prices you will have to pay*. In order to help you get an accurate costing use the list on page 46 as a guide to the various items you might need to get started (not everyone will need all the items on the list, of course).

In addition you will of course need any equipment specific to your proposed business. Jot them down as you think of them during the planning stages.

Producing documents

You may think that figure 6 contains items you do not need. However, all of them could be justified. Your business image will be greatly enhanced, and therefore more likely to attract customers, for example, if you use an electric typewriter or a word processor to type your letters and quotations. Such machines are comparatively cheap, and will repay their costs quickly. If you want to appear professional they are vital.

A photocopier may also seem a needless expense. However, you are legally required to retain copies of all your financial records, and it is vital for your administration to keep copies of correspondence. Carbon paper in a typewriter provides adequate copies, but it is messy, and is not as accurate as photocopying, especially if you make mistakes! A table-top photocopier can be bought for around £400, is an extremely worthwhile investment and also saves time-consuming and costly visits to copy shops.

Transport

A car or van may not seem really necessary at first, but consider how you propose getting to customers, or to suppliers. Public transport may be feasible but it will be time-consuming. A car or van is virtually essential for most people who operate a business from home.

Filing

If you frowned at the four-drawer filing cabinet and thought one with two drawers would be cheaper, and would take up less space, think again. Business soon accumulates mounds of paper and a four-drawer filing cabinet is the bare minimum you should consider. It will soon fill up.

Telephone answering machine

If you think that a telephone answering machine is unnecessary, just imagine how many customers cannot get a reply when you are out, and who therefore call your competitors who are in! That represents lost business. An answering machine is a lifeline for self-employed people and should be at the top of your list of required equipment.

All the equipment has been listed because it will make many home-based business easier to operate. It will increase your efficiency and make you more profitable. Skimping on the supplies you need at the start will reduce your ability to work effectively, and so your business operation will be inefficient, making you less able to compete. However, don't go over the top and buy expensive items you don't need. A window cleaner will not need a word processor, for example!

Advertising and marketing

One start-up cost not yet mentioned is the expense of advertising and your initial marketing exercise. This will depend on the type of marketing and advertising you need. Obtain accurate quotations for the printing of advertisements, leaflets or posters, as well as the costs of advertising in the publications you want to appear in. Calculate the total costs based on the marketing plans you will write in the next section of your business plan.

Borrowing

The final item which needs to be listed in the section on start-up costs is the expense incurred in any borrowing you may need. The cash available to start the business may be insufficient and you may need loans to buy equipment, for example. The costs of such loans must be incorporated into start-up costs. All the high street banks provide loan repayment tables which show how much you would have to pay each month for specific levels of borrowing. Budget for at least the first three months of payments as well as any arrangement fees before expecting any income from your customers to support the loan.

Computer

Powerful business computers can now be obtained for less than £1,000 and could be a boon to your business, allowing you to organise your information, calculate your accounts, handle your promotional efforts, and so on. Many home-based businesses will be made considerably more efficient with the use of a computer, and you could therefore consider the purchase of one at the outset. If you do, incorporate the costs of purchase into your start-up costs and add the cost of purchasing computer disks, a printer, printer paper, and the storage boxes for disks.

Internet access

A business starting up these days will almost certainly want internet access. As well as providing a useful source of information, far greater than your local library, the internet is also a rich supply of potential customers. Added to that it is a useful place to obtain supplies, such as stationery and computing items. To gain access to the internet you will need a special device known as a modem (included with most computers nowadays). In addition, you'll need an account with an 'access provider' or 'internet service provider'. Many of these are now free of charge. One of the most popular is Freeserve and you can obtain a disk to get you going, free of charge from any branch of Dixons or PC World. Other free services are available and you can find them listed in popular internet magazines such as *.net* and *Internet Works*, available from most newsagents.

Listing all your needs

Now you need to write all your start-up costs into your business plan. First list the equipment and services necessary to establish your business. Then explain how you obtained the costs for all these materials. Say, for example, that the costs are averaged from three written quotations from leading suppliers, if that is how you obtained the prices. Also, add a small percentage to allow for inflation in between the time of obtaining the costs and starting up your business, and explain this addition.

Next list the items you want and the funds you need to buy them. Don't list every single item of stationery or equipment. These can be grouped together into 'Stationery' and 'Equipment'. Similarly, if you intend to buy a computer and its associated peripherals just list the price under 'Computing equipment'.

You will now have an overall total of your start-up costs. Point out at this stage that these costs exclude the funds required to pay for your own needs such as mortgage, heating bills, food and so on. All of these items will be dealt with in the cash flow forecast produced later in the plan. However, your advisers need to know what money will be needed simply to set up the business.

Marketing information

The next section of your business plan will explain where your customers will come from, how many you envisage, what prices they can be expected to pay, and how you plan to attract them. This section should include:

● a detailed list of potential customers — including the names and addresses of the most important ones
● a plan of campaign on how you will become known to such customers
● complete information on competitors — including addresses, strengths and weaknesses (see Chapter 2).

You will need to plan a marketing and advertising campaign, which might include:

● local newspaper advertising
● magazine advertising
● radio advertising

- television advertising
- posters
- leaflets
- brochures
- a public relations campaign.

The sort of marketing operation devised will depend on the type of business you are starting and the likely competition. If you are setting up a window-cleaning service, for example, a leaflet campaign to local houses may be sufficient, but if you intend starting a fashion design consultancy you may need to advertise nationally in the fashion trade press and in women's magazines. Chapter 6 will help you sort out the types of marketing exercises available if you want to learn more before committing yourself in your business plan.

Your cash flow forecast

A major part of your business plan will be the financial predictions of the first three years of the business. It is important to estimate your trade over a number of years so that a picture can emerge of your likely financial stability. The information needed in this section is the total anticipated expenditure for each year, and the likely income. Whilst this will only be an estimate, try to justify your figures. For example you might expect more customers in the second year, but expenditure might increase because you have to buy more raw materials and equipment to satisfy the increased demand. Make careful assessments of how you expect your business to grow, and translate that into figures. This will become your **cash flow forecast**.

Cash is not profit

A cash flow forecast is simply an estimate of the income and expenditure of your business over a given period of time — for example, a year. Remember that this is *not* a profit forecast. Profit and cash are two entirely different things in the business world — do not assume that having a lot of cash in hand means you have made a profit! Similarly, any profit you make might not be easily transferred into cash.

Format

For your business plan, you will need cash flow forecasts to cover the first three years. For each six-monthly period use a large sheet of paper broken up into fifteen vertical columns. The left-hand column contains various headings and categories. The right-hand two columns are for totals. The remaining columns are for the six months, with two columns

ITEM	1st Quarter	2nd Quarter	3rd Quarter	4th Quarter	TOTALS
Mortgage/rates	450	450	450	450	1,800
Capital costs	1,275	325	85		1,685
Loan repayments	240	240	240	240	960
Cash purchases	320	280	175	100	875
Services	460	300	270	200	1,230
Raw materials	1,225	200	1,225	150	2,800
Taxes	300	400	500	700	1,900
TOTAL PAYMENTS (A)	4,270	2,195	2,945	1,840	11,250
Cash sales	400	1,200	3,850	4,200	9,650
Credit sales	3,800	3,400	2,400	1,200	10,800
Other receipts			100		100
TOTAL RECEIPTS (B)	4,200	4,600	6,350	5,400	20,550
BALANCE (B-A)	(70)	2,405	3,405	3,560	9,300

Fig. 7. A quarterly summary cash flow forecast (£).

for each month. The first column in each month is for your **estimated** figures, and the second is for recording the **actual** figures, so that you can make a quick comparison.

Down the left-hand column list headings for your income and expenditure, with income in the top portion of the form, and expenditure below. Leave space at the bottom to calculate the difference between income and expenditure. In the income section have headings for items such as sales made, debts repaid and interest from deposit accounts. The expenditure you will make each month includes mortgage, rates, equipment and advertising.

Many banks provide ready printed cash flow forecast forms to business customers.

Having made up the basic form, or used one supplied by a bank, estimate each month's income and expenditure and complete the form. Estimated income will be related to the number of customers predicted in the previous section of the business plan. Your monthly expenditure *should not be underestimated*. It is helpful to summarise your cash flow on a quarterly basis to provide a good 'snapshot' of your expected income and expenditure.

Once all this is down you will be able to summarise the data and calculate each year's estimated income and expenditure. Explain fully how you arrived at the final figures so that any professional adviser who reads your business plan will understand the basis of your calculations.

Final remarks
When the final section of the business plan is finished you can write the final sections of the document.

The last section of your business plan should describe where you expect your business to be in three years time from start-up. That doesn't mean where you physically expect it to be located, although if you do expect to move premises, say so. Your cash flow analysis will have provided the basic financial information, but you need to think carefully about what you want to have achieved at the end of three years.

Perhaps your aim is to be the most successful British freelance fashion designer. Alternatively, maybe your only ambition is to provide a regular income sufficient to provide some 'pocket money'. In either case, make your ambitions clear in your statement. Your advisers need a picture of your intentions and unless you tell them they will ask you what it is you are trying to achieve with your business. Use your cash flow forecast to explain the final figures at the end of three years, and also give some hint as to what you propose to achieve beyond the first three years of operating.

Your advisers will also want to know about any problems you are likely to encounter. These should include any risks you could face in operating the business, mentioning in particular:

● competition
● legal hazards
● family situations.

You will have gathered this information in your answers to questions in Chapter 2. You will need to include as much detail as possible and you must be honest. Do not try to fool your advisers!

The importance of planning ahead

Ask any professional adviser about the reasons for business failure and you will invariably be told that a lack of planning was involved. Don't cut any corners in preparing your business plan. You will need to spend hours planning, rewriting and replanning probably for some weeks before your document is finished. Even if you want to get your business up and running next week and think you can write your proposals overnight, do not be fooled.

Presentation of your business plan

Once you are satisfied with the content of the plan, consider its presentation. The plan you produce has two aims:

● to make sure *you* understand what you are trying to achieve and how you intend to achieve it

● to attract the financial help and advice of others.

Very few home-based businesses can begin without some external assistance. At the very least you will need a bank account. To get a business account your bank manager will want to see your business plan — so make sure your plan is an attractive and easy-to-read document. If your plan is tattily presented, or handwritten you'll give your bank manager the impression that you're a slapdash individual with no real professionalism. Would *you* lend money to such a person?

Get your document produced as professionally as possible. It must, at the very least, be neatly typed on one side of a sheet of A4 paper only with wide margins and clearly identifiable sections. If possible, include as many professional-looking diagrams and charts and pictures as you feel are appropriate. This might cost you, although a desktop publishing bureau will be considerably cheaper than a type-setting firm.

USING YOUR BUSINESS PLAN

The main function of your business plan will be as presentation to potential investors. Most people starting their own business will have to borrow at least some money in the initial months, and your business plan will show potential investors that you are serious about your business. The most likely source of finance at this stage will be your bank (see page 64), but there are other sources you should consider:

- personal funds
- friends and relatives
- private investors
- building societies
- finance house (beware of high interest rates!)
- government schemes.

Government schemes

These are worth particular consideration as an alternative or supplement to borrowing from the bank, because there are an ever-increasing number of schemes to encourage small businesses. Contact the Training Agency or the Small Firms Information Service for more details, but one scheme is worth mentioning here.

The **Small Firms Loan Guarantee Scheme** is a scheme whereby the Government will guarantee a large proportion of a bank loan which is needed to start a business. This is particularly helpful for someone who might normally have problems obtaining a loan, perhaps because of a poor track record.

An excellent source of advice on Government support is the local Business Link. You will find your Business Link in the *Phone Book*. Or use the internet site at: www.businesslink.co.uk.

But remember, for either scheme, you must have a convincing business plan to prove to the authorities you are going to make your ideas work.

CASE STUDY: THE PETCARE HOTEL

The **Petcare Hotel** is the name of a fictional home-based business proposed by Angela Petcare. Miss Petcare is 22 years old and a qualified veterinary receptionist. She has GCE A Levels in Biology and Chemistry, both grade B, which were obtained at Smalltown Comprehensive School in June 1988. Miss Petcare also has three years' work experience in a busy veterinary surgery. She worked for Messrs. Beagle and Bugle of 27 The High Street, Smalltown. This is Smalltown's largest veterinary surgery and serves a catchment area of 16,000 homes. Miss Petcare's responsibilities at Beagle and Bugle included booking appointments and managing the visiting diary. She also dealt with telephone enquiries about pet care and grooming and dispensed medicines prescribed by the vets and nurses. She has attended five separate residential training courses on dealing with animals, and has specialised in the care of small pets, particularly hamsters, gerbils, mice, rabbits and budgerigars.

The Petcare Hotel

Miss Petcare intends opening an 'hotel' for small pets, such hamsters, rabbits, mice, budgerigars, and gerbils. The hotel would look after them whilst owners were away on holiday, or for any other reason unable to look after their animals. The service would complement existing boarding kennels which are for cats and dogs.

To run such a small pet hotel the proprietor would, in addition to business skills, require a knowledge of animal health, be confident in handling small pets and understand aspects of pet care such as grooming, cleaning and feeding. Miss Petcare is competent in all these areas of animal care as a result of experience gained working in a veterinary surgery. She is prepared to learn the basics of the business side by attending night school, and has already booked courses on administration and book-keeping, run by the Smalltown Adult Education Service during weekday evenings at the Smalltown Comprehensive School. The book-keeping course leads to examination by the Royal Society of Arts Stage One Book-keeping Certificate. The business administration course leads to an examination which is certified by the Smalltown Chamber of Commerce. Each course last twelve weeks and each session for two hours. Miss Petcare therefore aims to obtain 48 hours' tuition in basic business finance and administration at her own cost.

Location

The Petcare Hotel would be run from an existing extension to her parents' five-bedroom detached home in Smalltown. The extension comprises of a centrally heated room of 220 square feet and an unused garage. Both are separated from the main house by a hallway and have electricity and hot and cold running water. There is a large sink in the room adjoining the garage and a telephone point and the garage includes 48 cubic feet of available cupboard space. Miss Petcare plans to house the animals in the centrally heated room, and store the necessary equipment and food in the garage. Her office will be a screened off section of the main room. Customers will be able to approach the establishment via a separate pathway and door so that the household is not disturbed. This pathway is not close to any neighbouring properties so visitors will not annoy nearby residents. The driveway approaching the garage is sufficiently large to take five cars so no street parking for clients will be necessary, thus further reducing the possible annoyance to neighbours (see diagram).

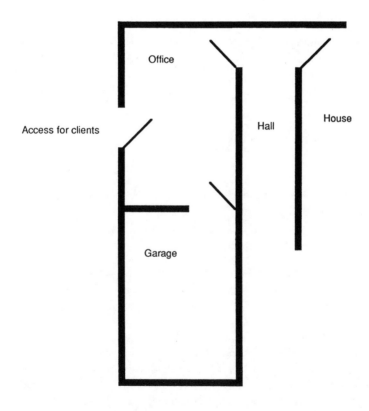

Fig. 8. The layout of a work area.

Finances

The current financial position of Miss Petcare is outlined below:

Item	Amount
Current Assets	
Savings (Cash at Smalltown Building Society, A/C No 12345)	750.00
Car (1984 Vauxhall Nova)	2,750.00
Monthly income	
Gross Salary	500.00
Building society/bank interest	5.00
Subtotal	505.00
Monthly outgoings	
Tax/NI	109.00
Rent paid to parents	60.00
Clothes	50.00
Records	35.00
Meals/drinks	80.00
Life assurance premium	10.00
Miscellaneous	40.00
	384.00
Excess income per month	121.00

Fig. 9. Example of monthly personal financial situation.

She therefore has funds of £750 available which would be used during the initial start-up of the business. She could also save a further £363 during the next three months before leaving her present employment.

Start-up costs

The expected start-up costs include the cost of a loan for the purchase of equipment. The total cost of £1,960 includes the provision of office equipment, a computer, stationery, printing, advertising and initial marketing and animal food supplies. (No animal cages are required at this stage since owners will be expected to provide their own). The chart below shows prices estimated from written quotations and price lists provided by potential suppliers.

Item	Cost
Desk	75.00
Filing cabinet	110.00
Telephone/answering machine	175.00
Headed notepaper/business cards	45.00
Envelopes	20.00
Postage stamps	38.00
Miscellaneous stationery	60.00
Small computer and printer	573.85
Computer consumables	48.65
Advertising	297.00
Direct mail shot	195.00
Posters	69.00
Animal foods	75.00
Loan charges (first three months)	178.50
Total	1,960.00

Fig. 10. Example of a budget for start-up costs.

The Petcare Hotel's customers are expected to come from the Smalltown area, which has 75,000 households. An estimated 40% of householders own pets, with 30% of these pets being the small animals likely to want the services of the Petcare Hotel, so the Smalltown are has an estimated 9,000 small pets. If owners go away on holiday for an average of two weeks each year, there will be an estimated 354 families who own small pets away on holiday every week. If 10% of these choose to use the services of the Petcare Hotel, Miss Petcare can expect to house around 35 pets each week. She is aware of the likely seasonal fluctuation in her business and has decided to take her own holidays during the winter months, between the summer season and the skiing season. Miss Petcare would also use the slack periods of business during winter to repair her equipment, arrange new stocks and plan promotional and marketing activities. The winter months will also allow Miss Petcare to visit homes of clients to advise on animal health and provide grooming.

The potential market
Most of the potential customers are thought to be in their late 20s to late 30s with small children, having reasonable amounts of disposable income. Smalltown is one of the UK's fastest growing new towns and

has a high proportion of young high earners working in new technology and financial sectors. According to the Smalltown Development Agency individuals in Smalltown have a higher proportion of disposable income than any other town in Small County. This means that the potential customers of the proposed Petcare Hotel would have funds available to spend on accommodation for their animals whilst away on holiday.

Advertising

Miss Petcare intends to attract her customers with a leaflet campaign in the town, using the Household Delivery Service of the Post Office. She plans to advertise in three local newspapers — *The Smalltown Guardian, The Smalltown Evening News* and *The Advertiser* — as well as providing posters for the nine veterinary surgeries in the area. She will also be sending press information on her enterprise to local newspapers and the town's radio station, hoping to gain beneficial editorial coverage. Her fiancé is a journalist on *The Smalltown Guardian* and will be able to write the press release so that it has maximum impact.

Cash flow forecast

The cash flow forecast shows that in the first year the income is projected at £12,000. Her expenditure in this year is estimated at £5,560, including the start-up costs, thus providing a net income of £6,440. The following two years are estimated to provide a net income of £6,980 and £11,575.

Within three years Miss Petcare wants to make The Petcare Hotel the most successful small pet-caring agency in Smalltown. She expects to expand the business gradually over the first three years but proposes a major expansion in the fourth year. This would mean buying larger premises, which would be financed by a mixture of borrowing and increased custom. At the end of five years Miss Petcare expects the hotel to be one of the most important services provided to families in the Smalltown area. She intends investigating the possibility of franchising the concept during year six, with a long-term aim of running a series of Petcare Hotels throughout the country.

Potential problems

The only problem which Miss Petcare envisages is in the provision of extra space and cages. This accounts for extra expenditure in year two, which explains the lack of any real increase in net income from year one to year two. Miss Petcare has the full support of her parents and the neighbours are co-operative. She also has the support of her current employers who have agreed to become the veterinary consultants to the practice and to provide support and advice when necessary. There is no mortgage on the property, and the appropriate authorities have been approached with regard to any licensing requirements. The planning department have said that a change of use certificate could be required and that since the dwelling is in the centre of Smalltown in a mixed residential and commercial area there should be no difficulty in obtaining the necessary approvals.

Miss Petcare does not anticipate any other difficulties in starting up her business. She intends leaving her current employment in February so that her business can be organised and marketed prior to the summer months when most of her custom can be expected.

National Westminster Bank PLC   **Cashflow Forecast For**

Branch   ANYTOWN   name of company, firm etc

Enter month	MARCH		APRIL		MAY	
	Projected	**Actual**	Projected	**Actual**	Projected	**Actual**
Receipts						
Sales – Cash			500 – 00		750 – 00	
Sales – Debtors			250 – 00		350 – 00	
Loans	1000 – 00					
Other receipts	1000 – 00					
A Total receipts	2000 – 00		750 – 00		1100 – 00	
Payments						
Cash purchases	33 – 00		20 – 00		50 – 00	
To creditors						
Wages and salaries (net)						
PAYE/NIC						
Capital items	934 – 00					
Rent/rates						
Services	561 – 00					
HP/leasing repayments						
Bank/finance charges						
Loan repayments	178 – 00		178 – 00		178 – 00	
Stationery	174 – 00				50 – 00	
Animal food	75 – 00		100 – 00		150 – 00	
VAT (net)						
Corporation tax, etc						
Dividend						
B Total payments	1960 – 00		298 – 00		428 – 00	
Opening bank balance			40 – 00		492 – 00	
Add to B if overdrawn Subtract from B if credit						
C Total	1960 – 00		258 – 00		(64 – 00)	
D Closing bank balance (Difference between A&C)	40 – 00		492 – 00		1164 – 00	

Fig. 11. A cash flow forecast

: PETCARE HOTEL   From MARCH   To AUGUST

JUNE -		JULY		AUGUST		Total	
Projected	Actual	Projected	Actual	Projected	Actual	Projected	Actual
1000 - 00							
350 - 00							
1350 - 00							
50 - 00							
150 - 00							
178 - 00							
200 - 00							
578 - 00							
1164 - 00		1936 - 00					
(586 - 00)							
1936 - 00							

partially completed for the Petcare Hotel.

4

Choosing Your Professional Advisers

Every business needs professional advisers from time to time. No-one has enough experience to know the answers to every single problem that crops up. Even if you are highly skilled or experienced in your chosen field, you will still need advice from outsiders. External sources of advice are very important for people who work at home. It is easy to fall into bad habits and poor methods of working without the presence of colleagues and bosses. Also, since most people starting a business from home have little if any business administration or financial knowledge, it is a good idea to ask for professional advice as early as possible so that the venture sets off on the right foot.

YOUR BANK MANAGER

The first person you are likely to approach is someone who will prove to be an invaluable and important contact in your business life — your **bank manager**. At the very least you will need him to approve your application for a special bank account for your business earnings, and you will probably need advice on loans and other financial assistance. Getting to know your bank manager is a vital aspect of your business — requests for financial support are more likely to be met with enthusiasm if the manager knows about you and your business than if you are an unknown entity.

Many people think bank managers only become involved with customers if they owe money. In fact, most of the people a bank manager sees in an average day are businessmen and women who need advice, information and assistance. The bank manager is not an ogre but a highly experienced individual with a wide knowledge of finance and business. Bank managers also have a network of other consultants and professionals whose knowledge they can draw on for advice and assistance should your requests be unusual. Banks also employ their own specialists who concentrate on particular types of customer. For example, all banks have specialist managers who understand the needs of the self-employed and small businesses. So if your branch manager does not have sufficient specialist experience in your field there is likely to be someone within the bank's region who can help. However, always begin by contacting the branch manager of the bank you want to use.

Which bank is for you?
Choosing a bank seems complicated with the wide variety of accounts now available. If you are happy with your current banking arrangements then it is wise to have your business account there as well. However, do look around at the competition to see what is available. High Street banking is becoming increasingly competitive and the fight for business customers is intense. It is worth remembering too that the larger building societies also offer cheque accounts, so see what is on offer. Building societies are also open longer hours than most banks, but they have fewer cash card machines and cheques need ten days to clear, rather than three for the banks. However, the interest rates on deposit accounts are usually higher than those offered by the banks. So shop around, and ask yourself: What sort of account do you really need?

Specialist banking services
All High Street banks offer specialist services for small businesses and the self-employed and produce a whole range of informative booklets and leaflets for potential business customers. Even some building societies produce brochures and booklets for potential business customers. Get hold of as many of these brochures as possible from your local branches. Once you have read all of the literature you can decide which of the banks offers the kind of services you want.

The local branch?
In these days of electronic financial transactions and the ubiquitous fax machine it may seem unnecessary to choose a local branch. However, there are advantages:

● You can pop in and see the staff more easily.

● The manager can provide more personal help.

Bank managers form the hub of much local business activity and are able to pass on useful sales contacts to their clients as well as help assess local competition. Although the bank managers are forbidden to act as agents, they are able to help their customers by pointing them in the right direction to improve their business. There are extremely strict laws and codes of practice relating to the security of banking information and so the activity of clients is totally confidential. Even the courts are required to obtain injunctions to get information from a bank manager! So the manager will not act as a local publicity mouthpiece for your business, but should someone he meets want the services of products you sell, your name may very well be dropped into the conversation! The banks would probably deny that such information ever passes the lips of their staff, but the system has been established for centuries — and it's unlikely to change now!

Approaching the bank

Once you have decided which bank you want to use, make an appointment to see the branch manager. If the manager is not particularly well-acquainted with you or your finances, begin by writing a letter. Branch bank managers are extremely busy people and their personal assistants ensure that their appointments diary does not become cluttered with people who say they need to see the manager when they could get their demands met at the enquiry desk! The example on page 68 shows the sort of introductory letter you could write.

Notice that the letter is addressed to the manager by name. Do not write a 'Dear Sir' letter — the manager will think that you don't really care whether you bank at this particular branch or not. Get the name of the manager from the switchboard operator.

The sample letter clearly shows that Miss Petcare is looking for advice as well as a bank account. The letter is accompanied by the business plan so that the manager can see the details of the proposed business. This is the document that will help the manager decide whether or not you are the sort of customer the bank wants. A well thought-out business plan that shows steady growth in the business means more money flowing into the bank. However, the bank manager will also be looking for loopholes and likely problems with competition. Bank managers know a great deal about local businesses and are therefore in an excellent position to assess competing organisations. If your business plan has too many unanswered questions or has too many strong competitors you will be a bad risk for the bank since any money you borrow may not be paid back if your business fails.

If your bank manager likes the idea you put forward in your proposal and thinks that the bank could offer the services you need, he will invite you to the branch. Your initial appointment will probably only last for 30 minutes or so and you may well be passed on to one of the clerks to complete the appropriate forms.

Your first appointment

When you go to the bank for your first appointment, take along your business plan and any back-up financial information such as building society books and previous bank statements. If you already bank at the branch your manager's assistant will have prepared a profile showing the manager the flow of funds in and out of your accounts. This information allows the manager to assess how you manage your finances. People who frequently overdraw without permission are not going to be a good risk for a business account.

- Do you manage your personal finances well?
- Are you totally honest with the bank?
- Have you prepared your business plan?

If the answer is 'yes' on all three counts, you stand a good chance of becoming a business customer.

Occasionally, your first appointment at the bank may not be with the branch manager. Most managers deal with quite high-level lending and delegate new accounts to assistant managers or deputies. Some banks have small business specialists so your initial letter may be referred to this person. Do not be offended — many bank managers are happy to admit that dealing with small business customers and the self-employed is best left to the specialist within the branch who understand their needs more precisely.

Your business account
Once your business account has been opened you will probably receive:

- cheque book
- paying-in book
- cheque card (if required)
- letter of welcome
- details of services offered
- names of key staff at the branch for your requirements.

Write to the branch manager, or small business adviser, thanking them for their time and their help — whatever the outcome of the meeting has been. Make it clear that there is an open invitation to your premises. Bank managers like visiting their customers on their home ground as this gives them a much clearer picture of their work. If you make the first move, the manager is much more likely to respect you and your business, thus enhancing your reputation and status within the bank's list of clients. You will be able to reap the rewards of such a letter by having a manager who understands your business and is sympathetic to your needs.

[Date]

Mr Watkinson
The Manager
Anytown Bank
1 The High Street
Anytown

Dear Mr Watkinson

I am proposing to set up my own business based at my home. My plan is to set up an hotel for small pets which will care for hamsters, rabbits and so on while their owners are away on holiday. I have produced a detailed business plan for the first three years which is enclosed for your information.

I am currently seeking banking facilities and as you will see from the plan I will also need a loan of around £1,000 to help me with the start up finance. The costs of such borrowing have been taken into account in the cash flow plans which accompanying the business plan.

I would be grateful if I could come and see you to discuss my plans and the possibility of opening a business account at your branch. I would naturally be happy to hear your comments on my proposals and your suggestions for the best way to finance the start up costs.

I look forward to hearing from you.

Yours sincerely

Angela Petcare

Fig. 12. An introductory letter to the bank manager.

Getting the most out of your bank manager

- Be open and forthcoming.
- Be well-prepared with information and paperwork.
- Listen and be ready to accept the benefit of his/her experience and advice.
- Ask plenty of questions on both business and bank matters.

Complaining to the bank

If you have any complaints about your bank's service, mention your concerns to the branch manager or the senior official with whom you regularly have contact. If that does not achieve the required results write to the bank's local head office. If you are *still* not satisfied then contact the Banking Ombudsman. Tel: 020 7404 9944. The Ombudsman will investigate your case and decide if your grievance is justified. All of the main banks participate in the Ombudsman scheme and take note of the decisions made. However, a good rapport with your bank manager will prevent you having to take such drastic steps.

YOUR ACCOUNTANT

Although you do not *have* to use the services of an accountant, it is wise to do so. Accountants know how best to secure the maximum **tax relief**. They also understand the Self Assessment tax forms, which can be quite daunting for non-experts! This is a legitimate reduction you can make in your tax bill. Self- employed people are allowed to deduct a wide range of expenses from their overall tax liability and small businesses and partnerships can also benefit from similar deductions. However, the tax laws are complex, so the services of an accountant greatly simplify the procedure and ensure that you pay the absolute minimum amount of tax — so the cost of an accountant will almost certainly repay itself in your first year of trading. Also, remember that the fees an accountant charges are also tax deductible expenses! That means he can calculate your tax, charge you and so further reduce your tax liability!

Finding an accountant

Ask your bank manager to recommend a good accountant — every bank will deal with accountants in your area, and the manager will know the firm most suitable for you. Get three or four names if possible and then approach them for a scale of charges, and a list of services offered. The letter on page 70 shows the sort of information you need to give when approaching an accountant.

[Date]

Mr A J Smythe
Senior Partner
Smythe, Smythe and Smythe
3 The Cuttings
Smalltown

Dear Mr Smythe

I am planning to start my own business based at my home and I am currently seeking an accountant to help handle my financial affairs. I have been given your name by Mr Watkinson of the Anytown Bank.

The business I am starting is described in the enclosed business plan. In essence I intend to offer a pet care service to local families. I envisage doing all my own book-keeping and VAT returns. I am seeking an accountant who could provide on-going advice and produce my annual accounts and deal with the Inland Revenue on my behalf.

Naturally, I have written to other accountants in Smalltown and Anytown but I hope to make a decision on who to appoint within the next three weeks. So I would be grateful if you could let me know as soon as possible whether or not you could take on my business and the fees you would charge for the work I have outlined.

Yours sincerely

Angela Petcare

Fig. 13. An introductory letter to an accountant.

Another alternative is *Yellow Pages*. Apart from a comprehensive list of accountancy firms in your area, you will also find a list of all the members of the Institute of Chartered Accountants and the Chartered Association of Certified Accountants. More information on choosing accountants can be obtained from these two organisations. The Institute of Chartered Accountants is at PO Box 433, Chartered Accountants Hall, Moorgate Place, London EC2P 2BJ. If you are in Scotland write to the Institute at 27 Queen Street, Edinburgh EH2 1LA. The Chartered Association of Certified Accountants can be contacted at 29 Lincoln's Inn Fields, London WC2A 3EE.

How much do accountants cost?

Unlike bank managers, accountants charge for their advice by the hour, typically £50 to £120, but often more in bigger firms in large cities. Don't be afraid to ask how much they charge — as you can see in the sample letter, a simple request for a scale of charges is enough. Naturally, the fees you pay depend upon the amount of time needed on your accounts. If you ask your accountant to perform all of your weekly book-keeping you will be charged a great deal more than someone who only uses an accountant to prepare the annual accounts for tax purposes. Starting a business at home usually involves keeping a close eye on your finances — so it is probably a bad idea to ask an accountant to perform your book-keeping because:

● it will increase your costs

● you will become detached from your financial situation.

Even your accountant himself will probably warn you against it! Home-based businesses usually benefit from using an accountant to prepare the annual accounts, deal with the tax authority's queries about your affairs and generally provide advice and information during the year as you need it. Accountants will not wish to meddle in your affairs — they will simply complete your accounts as requested, providing it is within the law and that the various codes of practice to which they must adhere are satisfied. An accountant will not try to tell you how to run your business, though if asked for advice he will give a balanced view of your affairs. Naturally, you do not have to accept the advice you are given — but you will have to pay for it!

Keeping your accountant informed

A good relationship with your accountant is vital. You will want the best advice you can get for your money, and he can only provide the right advice if he has enough information about your business. Simply preparing your annual accounts will not give him enough background on your business to enable a fair assessment of your requirements. So keep your account up to date with the results of your endeavours. Every three months write to him with the latest information on your business. The letter on page 74 shows the sort of data you should give. This will help establish a clear picture in his mind about your business — which will, in turn, mean that you get the best advice available and will also ensure that your accountant remembers who you are. Simply sending your books in once a year will not be enough in a busy accountancy office!

Presenting your books

Keep your books up to date. If your books are untidy, incomplete and inaccurate your accountant will need to spend more time preparing your accounts. That time will cost you money and will also annoy him. If your books are neat and kept efficiently he can complete the work quickly and simply. That is a sure way of helping to establish a professional image with him. Like bank managers, accountants can drop names into conversations. If you maintain your professional image your business could be boosted as a result. Scrappy books and unordered receipts will mean that your accountant is unlikely to recommend you to anyone. If you follow the advice in Chapter 9 about book-keeping you can keep your accountancy bill low as well as establishing a good reputation. Remember that a good proportion of business is achieved by word of mouth recommendation. A good relationship with your accountant would work wonders!

Computerising your accounts information

One way of keeping your accountancy costs down and your tax office happy is to computerise your accounts. The various programs that are available all do 'double entry' book-keeping, making sure that your details are correct. The most popular 'small business' accounts programs include *QuickBooks* and *Sage Instant Accounting*. You can find these on sale in shops such as PC World. However, choose an accounts package that meets your specific needs and also is approved by one of the accountancy bodies. Such approvals are shown on the packaging when they apply.

Complaining to your accountant

If you are not satisfied with the services of your accountant or want to dispute the charges then you should write immediately to the individual concerned to express your worries. If you do not get any response to this you should complain to the senior partner in the accountancy practice. If you are still not satisfied contact the relevant professional body, listed earlier in this section.

YOUR LAWYER

If you think there may be any legal difficulties in using your home as business premises or if you foresee any other legal problems, seek legal advice immediately. Although, hopefully, you shouldn't need to use legal services as frequently as an accountant or bank manager, it is always wise to establish a good relationship with a local firm of solicitors. Usually your bank manager and accountant will be able to advise on a suitable solicitor, but if in doubt contact the local branch of the Law Society, which can advise you. You can get the address from your local Citizens Advice Bureau (listed in *Yellow Pages* under 'Information Services') or from the Law Society, 113 Chancery Lane, London, WC2A 1PL. Tel: 020 7242 1222.

When you set up your home-based business it is a good idea to get in touch with a commercial solicitor. Your family lawyer, if you have one, may not specialise in commercial law so ask for the help of someone who has a particular interest in the affairs of small business. You will probably need legal advice on planning, contracts, employment, consumer protection, finance and intellectual property. A small legal firm which deals solely in conveyancing and divorce cases will probably not have the depth of knowledge and experience that you need, so make sure that the firm you choose is one which has specialists in commercial law. If your business has specific governing laws, look for a solicitor who knows this area — for example, if you are writing and publishing from home your lawyer should be familiar with the complexities of libel and copyright. A letter of introduction will help you find the right lawyer. When you have, meet him to talk over your initial plans for your business. You need to know if you will be breaking any laws or restrictions before you start. If you start a business from home *without* legal advice you will be taking a number of risks (see Chapter 2).

Meeting your lawyer

When you meet your lawyer for the first time, take a copy of your business plan together with any other relevant documents, such as copies of mortgage agreements and property deeds. Give the solicitor the name and address of your accountant and of your bank. This information will be kept on file and will be useful if these three specialists need to discuss

Mr A J Smythe
Senior Partner
Smythe, Smythe and Smythe
3 The Cuttings
Smalltown

Dear Mr Smythe

It is now six months since I started operating the Petcare Hotel and I am very pleased with the way matters have progressed. Naturally, I am very grateful for your advice and encouragement when I was setting up the business. I am quite sure I would have made mistakes in my VAT calculations without your help.

So far the Hotel has attracted more business than I had originally anticipated. Turnover to date is £12,540 with a gross profit of £8,670. As a result I have re-appraised my situation and rewritten my business plan for the next three years. A copy is enclosed for your information. Obviously, I would be happy to hear your comments on my proposals.

So far I have managed to maintain a good degree of credit control and only a tiny proportion of customers fail to pay in advance. I had anticipated having one third of my invoices unpaid in any one month but the actual figure is only 10%. Obviously this has improved my cash flow position and this is reflected in the new business plan.

I hope all this information is useful for your records but please do not hesitate to call if there is anything else you would like to know.

Yours sincerely

Angela Petcare

Fig. 14. Keep your accountant informed of your progress with a letter like this at regular intervals.

your situation — although the chances are they have had business contact with each other many times before you came along!

Your initial appointment with your lawyer will last about 30 minutes and you will not be given any definite answers! Solicitors like to consider their replies before committing themselves. The law is extremely complex and in many instances there is not a simple answer to a particular problem. Your solicitor will need to consider all aspects of your proposed venture before providing advice — but the advice provided will be legal, honest and decent. If they provide faulty advice they can receive severe reprimands and can even be struck off the Law Society's Register, making it impossible for them to continue working as a solicitor. So don't expect an instant decision. Your solicitor will probably need a week or so before writing with suggestions and advice for your new business.

When you have received a reply, write a letter of thanks to the solicitor, making it clear that you will keep the firm in touch with your activities. Hopefully, you won't need to contact your lawyer too frequently. However, if the firm does not have regular information about your business on file it will be less able to offer constructive advice; so make sure that at least once a year you update the company on your business activities. A letter similar to the accountant's letter on page 74 would be fine. If you use a solicitor to help with your financial affairs, such as debt collection, it is also a good idea to provide a set of annual accounts for their records.

How much do solicitors cost?

Like accountants, solicitors charge for their advice and work. You will generally be charged around £50 to £120 per hour of work in provincial firms. Larger legal practices in big cities will cost much more and fees of £300 per hour are not unknown. You will also be charged for letters, telephone calls and fax messages. Ensure that you get a scale of charges from your solicitor on your first visit. Good firms of solicitors will have a printed form with details of charges on it. Be wary of a solicitor who is not forthcoming about the fees he charges. Honesty works both ways in a business relationship. Your lawyer will expect total honesty from you so it is only fair that you should expect the truth about the fees you will be charged.

Complaining to your lawyer

If you have any need to complain about the services you receive from your lawyer, write and complain as you would to your accountant. If you still receive no satisfaction, write to the senior partner of the legal

[Date]

Mr A White
Managing Director
Whitewash PR
24 The High Street
Anytown

Dear Mr White

I run the Petcare Hotel in Smalltown and I am currently seeking some public relations assistance. The Hotel provides short-term caring facilities for small animals such as rabbits, hamsters and gerbils. It is aimed at families going on their holidays who want someone to care for their pets while they are away.

My current difficulty is that even though business is booming I need some public relations advice and assistance. I do not have sufficient time myself to prepare brochures and press releases or to mail these to the appropriate recipients. I am therefore seeking a PR consultancy which will perform this work for me. Essentially I required someone to write a brochure about the hotel and to distribute this to potential customers via veterinary surgeries and pet shops. I also would like some press coverage of the work of the hotel.

I would be grateful if you could let me know the sort of charge you would make for this work and whether you could start during next month. Naturally I have written to other PR agencies and I would hope to appoint one during the next two weeks so I would be grateful for your early reply.

I look forward to hearing from you.

Yours sincerely

Angela Petcare

Fig. 15. Approaching a consultant for help.

practice in question. If that still achieves nothing, write to the Law Society which can use its own disciplinary procedures.

OTHER PROFESSIONAL ADVISERS

Lawyers, accountants and bank managers are the three mainstays of professional advice for any business. However, there are other professional advisers which you may need from time to time. These are usually **consultants** and they provide specific advice and information on a whole range of business activities. There are, for example, marketing consultants, public relations consultants, computer consultants, management consultants, and financial consultants. Unless your business is particularly large or complex you are unlikely to need them very often — and they are often expensive. A reasonably sized public relations consultancy for example could charge as much as £750 per hour for the services of a senior consultant! Even self-employed consultants can charge around £50 to £70 per hour and sometimes much more.

Choosing and using consultants

If you decide that you do need some extra professional advice, such as help with marketing, get some written quotations for the work you want done. A letter like the one on page 76 is the sort of thing you should send. Then read the reply very carefully and inwardly digest the small print! Again, the rules about complete honesty apply; a public relations consultant, for example, will not be able to get the best publicity for your organisation if you are not truthful about your business.

Most home-based businesses can probably survive pretty well without spending hard-earned cash on consultancy services. Sometimes you will need specialist advice, such as when you decide to computerise your activities, but generally you can cope well enough without having to develop the sort of relationship you need with your three main professional advisers — your bank manager, accountant and solicitor.

CHECKLIST

To get the most from your professional advisers:

● Be totally honest with them.

● Keep them regularly updated about your business affairs.

● Arrange occasional social meetings, such as lunches or evening drinks.

5

Starting Your Business

Having completed your business plan, talked it through with your advisers, and got the professional back-up you require, you will probably be very excited at the prospect of being able to launch your home-based business at last and earn some money working for yourself. However, you still need to take one or two more decisions. It may seem tiresome but planning is essential and skipping any steps now will only bring trouble in the future.

CHOOSING A BUSINESS NAME

If you haven't done this already, you must now decide on the **name** under which you will trade. You can choose to operate under any name you want, provided it's legal. You cannot, for example, start manufacturing watches under the name 'Rolex'. The existing Rolex company would be understandably upset, and would be able to use the laws of **passing off** to obtain financial compensation from you, and forbid you from manufacturing under that name again (even if your real name *is* Rolex). The basis for their claim would be that your customers might believe that the products they purchase from you are manufactured by the larger, more established company when in fact they are not. Similarly, you cannot use any name which is a **registered trade mark** or **service mark**, and you should avoid any names which may confuse you with the competition.

Trade marks

Trade marks provide a considerable degree of protection for companies and ensure that no-one else can copy the name since there are severe legal penalties for doing so. Service marks are similar, except that they apply to services rather than products. Other companies protect their interests by using trade marks and service marks and so prevent you from using their names. You can use the system yourself and trade mark your products or get a service mark for your company name. To get either you will need to apply to the Patent Office, Concept House, Cardiff Road, Newport NP9 1RH. Tel: (01633) 814000. The details of applying are complex and are explained in various leaflets available from this address.

There are also **Trade Mark Agents**, listed in *Yellow Pages,* who can provide advice and information on applying for marks to protect your business. However, applying for a trade or service mark can be a time-consuming and costly business. Check that you *really* need this level of protection before you enter into any kind of agreement.

Most businesses which start from home trade under their own name, so there should be no need to protect that by using a trade mark or service mark! The computer consultant Brian Armstrong for example, is hardly likely to want to trade under the name of his neighbour Doreen Duncan, who offers secretarial services!

Choosing an original name

However, you may need to consider trading under another name if yours is difficult to remember or say. If you have umpteen syllables with plenty of zs or xs in your surname your customers may find it a problem. Calling your company something short and snappy helps them get in touch and also ensures that your name can be more easily passed on by word of mouth.

Legislation concerning trade names

Since 1982, self-employed people have been free to work under any business name they like. If you do not operate under your own name, the law requires you to display your own name on the premises to which you invite customers and on your headed notepaper, quotations, invoices and all other official documentation. You do not have to put your own name on business cards and compliment slips, but this could prove severely limiting as your customers and potential customers would not know who to contact.

Final precautions

Check that no-one else runs a comparable business under the same or similar name — similarities will lead to a loss of business because potential customers will be confused over which company is which. Check telephone directories, business guides and advertisements for possible conflicts (if you have done your preparatory work properly you will have identified the names of all your competitors already). When you have decided on a name, tell your bank manager so that your business account can be opened with the correct title. Of course, if you have been able to decide upon a business name *before* writing your business plan so much the better — but leaving the naming of your business until you are about to begin means that you will have identified all the possible competition and so have avoided potential conflicts. Ideally your business name should be:

- short
- easy to remember
- easy to spell
- easy to say.

One final tip — using your own name means that people will remember the name of the person in charge!

DECIDING YOUR BUSINESS STATUS

At this stage you will also have to decide the status of your enterprise. There are three options available to you:

- sole trader
- partnership
- limited company.

Each of these has its advantages and disadvantages but most businesses run from home are operated on a **sole trader** basis.

Sole trader basis

As a sole trader, you are **personally liable** for any debts incurred by the business. If your business fails, so does your personal financial standing. However, there are considerably advantages:

- You can deduct the vast majority of your business expenses from your income, thus reducing your tax bill. You can even claim a proportion of the heating and lighting costs as legitimate business expenses. However, if you own your own home, try not to use one room wholly for business purposes, as you will be liable to pay Capital Gains Tax on any future sale of the property.

- You are not restricted by the laws governing any other business status.

- You do not have to submit complex accounts to Companies House.

- You do not have to hold shareholders' or directors' meetings and keep strict records of the proceedings.

In short, the sole trader can simply set up and get on with it.

Partnership status

A **partnership** has the advantage that there will be at least two people — and up to twenty — sharing the work and providing the start-up cash. A partnership agreement must be drawn up properly by a solicitor if each partner is to be protected from any wrongdoings by the other. But, if a partnership results in debts, and one partner disappears, the remaining partner could be responsible for *all* the debts. Partnerships can work, but most professional advisers do not recommend them, except in very specific circumstances. Anyone setting up a business in their own home would be strongly advised to steer clear of partnerships. If you and a colleague wish to join in business together, it would probably be wiser to choose one of the following courses of action:

- Both trade as individuals in the same field, swapping contacts and potential customers, and thus sharing the workload as well as retaining your self-employed status.
- Form a company.

Limited company status

A **limited company** has the advantage of being considered as a separate legal entity from the people who own it. If your business gets into debt, it is the limited company which is initially in trouble and not you. However, this does *not* mean you can run your company into enormous debts, extracting all the profits for yourself — the law will stop you from doing this. You might also have to make a **director's guarantee** which would make you pay any debts the company incurs if the business becomes insolvent. For example, banks will often only lend money to companies if the directors agree in writing to repay personally any debts to the bank if the firm collapses.

Setting up a company

To set up a company:

- you need a registered office at which you display the name of your company
- you must be prepared to hold regular directors' meetings, and shareholders' meetings (if applicable), and keep accurate records of the proceedings
- you need to keep highly detailed accounts.

Ask your accountant for advice. Most companies are bought **off the shelf** — that is, you buy another company, already formed but not trading, and change its name. It sounds complicated, but is actually much simpler than forming a company from scratch. You accountant would purchase a company off the shelf from a **companies agent,** which forms companies and keep the documents 'on their shelves'. The name of the company is then changed and once your fees have been paid to Companies House you can start trading under the name of the company. The whole procedure takes up to a month and will cost around £250 including all your accountant's fees, the cost of the company and the payments which have to be made to Companies House. In return you will receive three documents:

- Articles of Association
- Memorandum of Association
- Certificate of Incorporation.

If you do decide to form a company, remember that the procedures for accounting are much stricter than for sole traders or partnerships. You will also have to become employed by the company if you draw a salary or fees, and pay both employee's and employer's National Insurance contributions. You will also pay Income Tax on the salary you draw from the company as well as Corporation Tax on any profits made by the company after paying out your salary and PAYE. So the financial organisation of a home-based company is more complicated than that of a sole trader. However, forming a limited company can have advantages. If you run a business which runs a risk of not being paid by your customers then you would *not* normally be personally liable for your company's debts caused by the lack of funds. You can pay yourself with dividends instead of salary fees, thereby saving National Insurance. Also some home-based businesses are more or less forced to be limited companies. Certain computer programmers, for example, cannot be given work from large contractors unless they run a limited company.

If in doubt, ask your professional advisers which business status is best for you.

SETTING UP YOUR WORKPLACE

Your next step is to set up your own office, or workplace, ready to start work.

Obtaining supplies

Your previous planning will really pay dividends now. You already have a shopping list of equipment, furniture and stationery produced for your business plan — now is the time to use it. Allow three or four days to do all your shopping. When writing your business plan, you obtained a number of written quotations from various suppliers for your costs estimate. You probably also have a number of price lists and catalogues. Now that you're really about to start your business, check the prices again and re-work your cash flow predictions if prices have gone up.

If your earlier planning revealed that you need additional facilities, such as running water or electricity, in your work area now is the time to get them installed. Arrange for any other work, like carpeting or decorating, to be done at this stage. Naturally, all of the costs for this work should have been included in your start-up plan and your cash flow forecast. If they weren't, or if you have discovered additional work that needs doing, recalculate your cash flow predictions.

Planning the office layout

When you have prepared the workplace and obtained your equipment, you can set up your office in just the way you want it. Consider the following tips:

- Place your desk near to a natural light source.
- Place any computers with their screens at 90° to the light source as this helps reduce glare.
- Hide all cables to avoid tripping.
- Organise your filing system now, rather than waiting for piles of paper to mount up.
- Arrange bookshelves so that important books are close to your desk for quick and easy reference.
- Ensure that the windows and doors have adequate security with proper locks.

CONTACTING THE AUTHORITIES

When you are ready to begin work, you *must* let the following people know that you intend operating your own business on a self-employed basis before you do anything else:

- Inland Revenue
- Department of Social Security.

You may also need to let the following organisations know about your business:

- HM Customs and Excise
- Data Protection Registrar.

Inland Revenue

Before you start trading, and depending on the business status you have chosen, make sure you have done the following:

- informed the Inland Revenue that you are becoming self-employed, *or*

- informed the Inland Revenue that you are forming a company, and arranged to have your income tax paid through Pay As You Earn by your company.

If you have a P45 from your previous job, it is your company's responsibility as your employer to return it to the Inland Revenue when you start work again. If you are self-employed, it will be one of the documents which you must submit to the Inland Revenue at the end of the tax year. This might also be a good time to find out about Corporation Tax and whether it applies to you.

Ask your accountant which Inland Revenue office to contact — he may even do it for you. You will probably find that the tax inspectors take a much greater interest in your financial affairs as a self-employed person than they ever did when you were employed! Generally, the PAYE system ticks along quite happily; however, people who run their own businesses may be tempted to hide their financial affairs from the authorities, hence the attention given to the self-employed and small businesses. Don't forget, the tax inspectors know the ropes — they know just how much profit, for example, a home-based flower arranger makes on average. If your profits are markedly different from the norm they'll want to know why! To be on the safe side, keep records of all communication between the Inland Revenue and your accountant. So at the outset it is probably wise to allow your accountant to contact the local tax office to inform them of your changed circumstances.

Department of Social Security (Contributions Agency)

You have to contact the Department of Social Security (DSS) to let them know that you will now be responsible for your own National Insurance contributions. Mention your National Insurance number in the letter. If you do not know this, check your last P60 (the form provided by your employer which states the amount of income received and tax paid in each tax year).

Self-employed

If you are to be self-employed the DSS will send you a leaflet and a form for the payment **Class 2** contributions. In the summer of 1999 these contributions were £6.55 per week. They are best paid by monthly direct debit from your business bank account.

In addition to Class 2 contributions, the self-employed are required to pay **Class 4** contributions related to their profits. These profits will be calculated by your accountant and paid at the same time as you pay your tax bill. Class 4 contributions are collected on behalf of the DSS by the Inland Revenue.

If you are self-employed and pay these National Insurance contributions, you are not entitled to the same benefits as an employed person. The self-employed cannot claim unemployment benefit for example, and sickness benefit is only payable if you can provide evidence of your earnings, such as your accounts and your tax returns.

Limited companies

If you form a limited company you don't pay Class 2 contributions, but instead pay two sets of National Insurance. The first will be the employee's Class 1 contribution which is deducted from your salary under the PAYE scheme. The second contribution is the employer's payment which you are also responsible for since your company employs you!

Full details of the various National Insurance contributions you must make when operating a small business can be obtained from publication FB30 *Self-employed* available from your local DSS office or Main Post Offices.

HM Customs and Excise

The Customs department will advise whether or not you should register for **Value Added Tax** (VAT). Your nearest office is listed under 'Customs and Excise' in the telephone directory. Let them know that you intend operating a business, and they will send you a pack of information on VAT. Particularly you need *Should I Be Registered for VAT?* (Leaflet 700/1), *The Ins and Outs of VAT* (Leaflet 700/15), *Keeping Records and Accounts* (Leaflet 700/21) and *The VAT Guide* (Leaflet 700). Your accountant will also have information on registering for VAT and may even complete the necessary forms for you if you wish.

● You *must* register for VAT if you believe that your gross turnover will exceed the figures laid down by the annual budget. For the 1999-2000 tax year the registration limit was £51,000. Anyone who is self-employed and who expects a total income above this level has to register. The current registration limit can be obtained from your local Customs office, or accountant.

If you think that your sales will exceed the current levels register as a VAT trader *now*. If you don't, and your sales do exceed the registration limits, the Customs department can make you pay *all* the VAT you ought to have collected from your customers in the previous year! If your sales actually come in below registration levels, there are no penalties. You can even voluntarily register for VAT despite knowing that your sales will be lower than the registration limits.

Adding VAT to your prices
Once you have registered for VAT you will be required to add the appropriate amounts to your prices. Some items are exempt from VAT, such as children's clothes and foodstuffs. Other items and services attract two different levels of VAT, either 0% or 17.5% (1999 rates). For example, books have a VAT rate of 0% but writers charge the publishers 17.5% VAT since this is the rate applied to the work of authors. All of the rates are explained in the *VAT Guide* and in various leaflets produced by HM Customs and Excise. Before you start, make sure that you know which rates apply to the goods and services you provide, and add that percentage to your invoices. Your financial records have to be kept in perfect order and bang up to date. VAT inspectors have the right to investigate your financial affairs and can fine you if your records are not kept according to their rules.

Don't be put off registering for VAT by these restrictions, or deliberately keep your turnover down to prevent yourself from being forced into VAT trading. This is extremely limiting on the success of the business since it reduces funds for expansion and development. The paperwork involved in VAT trading is not extensive — it simply involves calculating the amount of VAT due on each item of an invoice, calculating the amount of VAT you have paid on your own supplies and then filling in a one-sided form each quarter. You can get computer programs that do all the hard work for you, such as *QuickBooks* or *Sage Instant Accounting*. Some traders, who have been registered for more than one year and have a turnover of less than £300,000 can now apply for annual VAT accounting, making the whole operation even less time-consuming.

When you are registered for VAT you collect the tax on behalf of the

Government. In return you are allowed to deduct the VAT you have paid on the supplies and services you have used in doing your work. If, for example, you invoiced a total of £1,000 worth of VAT in any given quarter and spent £400 in VAT you would only pay £600 to HM Customs and Excise. In this way, registering for VAT actually helps reduce the price of your supplies by 17.5% in many instances. Another advantage of VAT registration is that you keep the money you collect for about three months, so it earns interest for you and not for the Government! The extra money in your account also creates a better overall financial picture of your business. Being VAT-registered also gives an image of professionalism and financial standing to your business. Traders who are not registered for VAT will, to some large customers, appear to be 'small fry' and not serious, committed business professionals.

The advantages of VAT registration

- You can reclaim all the VAT you pay on almost all goods and services used in your business.
- Your business appears to be much more professional if it is VAT registered.
- Your bank balance looks healthier since your income also includes the tax you collect.

The disadvantages of VAT registration

- Your prices are increased by the amount of tax you need to charge (this is only relevant if your customers are not VAT registered and so cannot reclaim the tax they pay to you).
- Your accounts must be extremely well kept.
- Your accounting paperwork is slightly increased.

Your accountant and the local Customs & Excise department will be able to help you decide whether or not to register as a VAT trader. In general, registering for VAT is much more helpful to the success of your business than attempting to keep your turnover below the registration levels for each year.

Data Protection Registrar

If you're going to use a computer in your business, and you expect to keep any kind of information about other people on it, such as an address list, you are required by law to register with the **Data Protection Registrar**. This costs £75, and puts your business on a central register of people who have information relating to individuals on their computers. Anyone who thinks that you have information about them can demand a copy of anything that you do have. (You can charge for the production of this material.) If you do not register the penalties are potentially enormous — fines are unlimited! To register, you need to fill in two simple application forms, available with a full information pack on data protection from the Data Protection Registrar, Wycliffe House, Water Lane, Wilmslow, Cheshire SK9 5AF. Tel: (01625) 545745.

Other officials

Don't forget that your business may also be the subject of special legislation. You may need to let other authorities know of your plans, and perhaps even get appropriate licences. For example, to make wine you need licences from both the local Customs department and the local magistrates (see Chapter 1). Whatever type of business you're in, make sure that you have contacted all the appropriate officials before you start trading, otherwise you could end up in trouble.

GETTING STARTED

When you have contacted all the relevant authorities you can finally begin work — although after all the planning, dealing with professional advisers and authorities, and sorting out your work-place, you'll probably need a few days off before you begin! Take a short break so that you can begin work well-rested and raring to go.

CHECKLIST

- Choose an effective, distinctive business name.
- Choose a solid business status — perhaps self-employed.
- Organise your workplace and institute a good filing system from the outset.
- Contact the Inland Revenue, the DSS, HM Customs and Excise and the Data Protection Registrar if necessary.
- Take a well-earned rest before you begin trading.

6

Attracting Customers

By this stage you will have completed most of the plans for starting your business. Now you can set about the real job of working. Well, not quite yet! There is still a bit more planning to do, although the groundwork of what you are now going to do will have been covered during the preparation of your business plan.

In your plan you will have written in some detail about the ways in which you intend attracting customers, the best ways of spending your money on publicity, as well as providing estimated budgets. Consequently, you have already done much of the foundation work for constructing a **marketing plan**. Now you can consider the fine detail.

YOUR MARKETING PLAN

A marketing plan lists the ways in which you intend to reach certain objectives. At this stage in your business career your primary objective is to attract customers. At a later stage you will need to construct further marketing plans to achieve different objectives. For example, you might want a marketing plan to:

- increase your customer base
- double your profits
- take customers away from your competitors
- sell off one particular product line
- increase the use of one particular service.

The principles of developing your marketing plan are basically the same. You write down your primary objective, and then outline the ways in which you propose achieving it. At this stage your primary aim is to obtain initial customers. You will also probably have a secondary aim, namely to ensure that customers repeat their orders.

Without attracting those first customers, and without getting their continued business, your enterprise would fall at its first hurdle! So the two-fold aim of your first marketing plan is an extremely important one.

ADVERTISING

Whatever kind of business you run from home, at some stage you will need to **advertise** your products or your services. If no one knows you exist, how are they going to buy anything from you? Advertising can be expensive, so you must ensure that you get value for money from it. It must be part of a planned campaign, and not just a haphazard attempt at spreading your name around.

You could consider any of the following advertising media:

- billboards
- cinemas
- internet
- local magazines
- local newspapers
- local radio stations
- national magazines

- national newspapers
- national television
- public transport
- regional television stations
- local radio stations
- shop windows
- specialist periodicals.

The best methods of advertising for you will largely depend on the sort of product or service you are offering, the area in which you are working, and your expected turnover. For example, if you have set up a home laundry service for working couples and expect to have an income of around £15,000, you would not consider advertising on national television! That would cause severe damage to your cash flow forecast. Your most appropriate method of advertising would be in local newspapers or newsagents' windows. However, if you are setting up a business manufacturing wine and which you estimate will have profits measured in hundreds of thousands of pounds, then television advertising may well be appropriate. The vast majority of home-based businesses will settle for less, though. TV advertising is extremely expensive and requires a large customer base to support it.

Choosing advertising media

As we have seen there are a number of different media in which you could advertise. Work through the following questionnaire to assess which media are the most suitable for your business.

1.   Is your business international, national or local?

2.   Is it a service-based business or one which will provide products?

3.   How much money have you set aside in your business plan for your advertising budget?

4. Will your customers come from the general public or from a more specialised and easily definable group?

5. Why should anyone want to buy your product or service?

6. Write a short profile of your customers, including age, sex, and likely income bracket.

Your answers to these questions will show the type of customers you expect, where they come from, and the sort of money they might spend. If they are members of the general public in your area your advertising should be restricted to affordable methods of local advertising such as:

● internet
● local newspapers
● local radio stations
● cinemas
● shop windows
● public transport.

If your customers are nationally based and come from the general public you should consider advertising in:

● national newspapers
● national magazines
● cinemas
● local radio stations on a national basis
● the internet.

If your customers are not members of the general public, but come from a definite subgroup, such as business computer users or professional caterers, you should consider advertising in:

● national magazines
● specialist periodicals
● the internet.

Of course there are no hard and fast rules, but your initial campaign should concentrate on the bare essentials, leaving any extra advertising outlets to a later date when you can afford them.

Planning your advertising
Once you have chosen the media in which you want to advertise, you can

plan your campaign. To do this you will need **rate cards** from the publications in which you want to advertise. This shows the prices you have to pay for various sizes of advertisement, and also gives details of how advertisements should be prepared. Another way of checking rates is to obtain a copy of the *Advertiser's Annual*. This contains a list of all the media and agencies, as well as other organisations which are helpful to advertisers. The media pages give a guide to the rates charged. The annual can be obtained from Hollis Directories, 7 High Street, Teddington, TW11 8EL (www.hollis-pr.co.uk).

Compare prices on the rate cards you receive — they will give details about the publication's circulation — and see which ones give value for money.

If you have to pay £150 for a half-page advert in a magazine which reaches 1,500 potential customers it will be less cost-effective than paying £340 for a half-page advert in a newspaper which reaches 3,750 people. Although the first example is cheaper, it actually costs 10p to get your advert to each potential customer. The second example would only cost 9p to reach each customer.

However, don't be fooled into believing that the media with the highest audiences are the ones you need to advertise in. For example, if your local newspaper reaches 35,000 people, and costs £350 for a quarter-page, it would not be as cost-effective as a publication which goes to only 12,000 people at £120, if this lower-circulation publication actually reaches more of your potential customers.

If you need to reach people who are earning large amounts of money, it is no good advertising in a down-market publication which is rarely seen by such individuals, no matter how high the circulation of that publication. So check the cost per reader/listener of each of the media you might use, but also check the audience profile to be sure that you really are getting value-for-money.

Value-for-money advertising

Use a sheet like the one opposite to estimate which advertising media are likely to work best for you.

Once you know where you want to advertise you will need to work out the **frequency** of your adverts. If yours is the sort of business which requires large numbers of customers spending small amounts of money you will need to advertise more frequently than people running businesses which charge large fees for complex projects which take a long time. In the early stages of your business development you should plan to advertise more frequently than you might later.

Once you have calculated the number of adverts you want you will be

Name of journal	Circulation (copies sold)	Page rate	Cost per 1,000	Life
Loamshire Gazette	35,000	£1,800	£51.43	Daily
Loamshire Advertiser	6,000	£ 160	£26.66	Weekly
Etc				

Fig. 16. Working out the real cost of advertising per 1,000 readers.

able to work out the **cost**. If this changes your cash flow predictions be sure to alter the forecast in your business plan, and check to see how it affects overall profitability.

Preparing your advertisements

When you have worked out how many adverts you want to place, and where, you can prepare their content. What you say in the adverts, and whether or not you use illustrations, will largely depend on the type of business, your personal choice, and the type of media in which you will be placing the adverts. Remember the following rules:

- Be honest.
- Be positive.
- Be concise.
- Use a clear headline.
- Convince the customer of the benefits of your products/service.

Writing adverts is a skill, and one which cannot be taught in a few paragraphs in a book such as this. However, there are several good books on the topic, most notably *How to Do Your Own Advertising*, by Michael

Bennie in this series, and *Do Your Own Advertising*, by Alistair Crompton (Hutchinson Business). These are aimed specifically at small businesses and include a wealth of advice on the practicalities of advertising.

Writing your own adverts

Most people who set up their own home-based business will not be able to afford the costs of using a design agency or an advertising specialist to produce their adverts. Instead, they will need to produce their own. Sadly, there are many examples of home-spun advertisements which are poorly written and badly presented. The examples below show how poor advertising can be if done incorrectly.

To produce your own well-written advertisement that will attract customers, sit down with a clear mind, a pad of white paper, a pencil and a copy of your business plan. Then write down all of the reasons why your business should prove attractive to your potential customers. Use your business plan as a reference document if you need any ideas or pointers. As you can see in the example on page 95 this list can be quite complex and heavily annotated. Once you have produced this list, take a second clean sheet of paper and prepare a summary of your thoughts, as shown on page 95.

The Petcare Hotel

Treat your pets to a holiday in the Petcare Hotel, Smalltown. While you take your holiday you can relax knowing that your small pets are being taken care of by fully trained staff. Contact us on: 0998-123.

The Petcare Hotel. Treat your pets to a holiday in the Petcare hotel, smalltown. Whil you take your holiday you can relax knowing that your small pets are being taken care off by fully trained staff. Contact us on: 0998-123.

Fig. 17. Make sure your advertisement is correctly spelt and designed — a bad advert is probably worse than none at all.

Gives them a rest.

Lets them have a worry-free holiday.

Cheaper than kennels.

LINKS
TO

No security worries by giving key to other people such as neighbours.

Convenient for all small-town residents.

Specific for small pets.

Run by specialists.

MAIN SALES POINTS

1. NO WORRIES FOR PET OWNERS.

2. PETS PAMPERED.

3. SMALL ANIMALS ONLY.

4. RUN BY SPECIALISTS.

Fig. 18. The first stage of writing an advert: Make a list
of your business's best selling points.

Selling the benefits
This summary will allow you to follow one of the basic rules of advertising — *The reader is not really interested in what you do or produce.*
What readers want to know is what they can get out of you *for their own
benefit.* In other words, your advertising must sell them something that
will be of real help to *them.* This is known as **benefit selling** and is one
of the most powerful forms of advertising. In TV adverts, the benefit is

often implied — if you drink this particular brand, you will be lively, happy, energetic and attractive to the opposite sex. But the principle is the same.

Advertising a home-based business is not like promoting a soft drink so your benefits will be much more obvious. If you offer a home-based typing service, for example, you can hardly imply that your work will make your customers more appealing to potential sexual partners! However, you can tell them that they will have more time for executive decision-making and the need for fewer staff typists, thus saving the staff budget, if they use your company. With the careful use of figures you can virtually prove such benefits. As a result the potential customer becomes interested in the possibility and wants to find out more — the advertisement has worked.

One key to benefit selling is that in the commercial world, one of the most important benefits you can provide is saving time. If your service can boast this put it at the top of your list of potential benefits.

Headlines
The benefits you list will form the basis for writing the **headlines** of your advertisements. The headline is the key to success in most advertising.

The Petcare Hotel

Release yourself from worry

Let your pet be pampered while you go away and relax

The Petcare Hotel caters only for small animals like rabbits, hamsters, mice, and gerbils. We will look after your pet with loving care while you relax on your holiday, or just while you take a small break.

Run by specialists in animal health care, The Petcare Hotel is the first facility of its kind in the area.

Let your pet have a holiday in style

**Contact: The Petcare Hotel
123 The Way, Smalltown, Largeshire, LG1 2SM
Tel. (0998) 123**

Fig. 19. Example of a simple, clear advertisement which could be produced in a high street copy shop.

This is the item which attracts the attention of the readers and gets them to read more. Without a good, informative, snappy headline, your advert will not attract readers and so it will be skipped. It will be a complete waste of money.

So, with your list of benefits on one sheet of paper use a clean sheet of paper to rewrite your benefits into a series of headlines. Look at the advertisements in the newspapers and magazines you have around the house. You will see that they are very short and often only have one or two words in large bold type. Don't be afraid to copy their style if you think it's successful!

Having written a series of headlines you can now start making some decisions. Which headline do you want to use? Choose one which will help introduce your business since none of the readers will have heard of your, your products or services before. Large established companies can assume that their name is already well-known, but small businesses cannot. Your headline must also provide interest and benefits. Often the best way is to split the headline into two separate items — one headline being the attention-grabbing benefit-seller and the other headline introducing your new company. Look at the example on page 96.

Writing the 'copy'
Having established the headline and the subheading you will need to write **the copy**. This is the text that provides the detail. Don't forget that people do not linger over advertisements like novels. They want a quick message, so don't provide too much detail. Provide just enough to whet their appetite for more. Be sure also that your copy contains the following items:

- a contact name if you are not trading under your own name
- the telephone number of your business
- your business address
- any other contact information such as fax or telex numbers
- an indication of prices if possible.

Without such information your advert will not be useful to the readers — if it's successful, they will actually *want* to know how much you are likely to charge or where to contact you.

Artwork
Having prepared all of the material you are now in a position to have the **artwork** for the advert prepared. Many local newspapers can do this on your behalf, but you have to stick to their choice of typefaces and their

decisions on layout. It is much better if you can get the work done by an agency such as a **copy shop** or **local printer**. To prepare the artwork for a simple advertisement, both would probably charge about £45. They would use their design skills to prepare your advert from the copy you provide, but they would not re-write the material nor would they offer advice on your proposed advert. To get that you would need to pay much more to a consultant in an advertising agency — probably not worthwhile for most home-based businesses. However, do get friends or relatives to have a look at your proposed advert so that you can get a second opinion. Working alone can give you tunnel vision and you might not notice some obvious errors or omissions.

Placing the order
Once your advertising artwork is produced, send it off with your order for space to the appropriate publications. Generally you do not pay for adverts until after they have been printed.

Newspapers and magazines will invoice you for carrying the advert after publication. Sometimes this can be months after the original advert appeared, so make sure that you budget for the expense and put the money aside.

You can always enhance your adverts with photographs or drawings. However, these will compete with top quality adverts from professional studios, so your graphics will need to be of extremely high calibre. It's probably wiser to leave out any ideas for graphics — unless your business is actually graphics-related — since any poor pictures will be damaging to the professional image you are trying to create.

Advertising on the internet

Simply having a 'presence' on the internet, your own 'web' site, is an advert in itself. Almost every Internet Service Provider allows you to have free pages on the web, so it is well worth taking up this offer. If you want a more professional presence, with your own 'domain name', you will need to buy commercial space. This can cost from £300 upwards per year. Whichever route you choose, your advert on the internet will be seen by people locally as well as around the world. So, make sure your first web page makes it clear who the material is aimed at, otherwise you might get requests for your gardening service from Australia! Lovely, but they probably won't pay your air fare as well as your hourly rate!

To make sure people see your advert, you need to promote your site within the internet itself. To do this you need to submit details of your internet site to the 'search engines'. There are various automatic ways of doing this. To make a start, visit the following web site:

www.linkexchange.com

Here you will find various ways of promoting your site and even advertising it on other web pages run by different people!

Radio advertising

If you want to produce radio advertisements then you will need specialist advice on writing them. You will probably only be able to afford a few seconds of airtime and this means that you must include the benefits and contact information, all in a snappy way. In a 15-second advert you could just squeeze in 45 words. That isn't very many, so the advert has to be extremely tightly written. It must also sound good, with a pleasant voice and perhaps some appropriate music. Take along your list of benefits and headlines to the commercials producer at your local radio station who will be able to use his or her skills to write your advert. Such services will be charged for, so ask for a rate card from the station first.

Other promotions

Apart from advertising there are all sorts of other promotional activities which you can try. However, you will need to decide which ones are the most cost-effective. This would be mostly common sense; if you want to sell secretarial services using a leaflet campaign, don't deliver the leaflets to houses on a residential estate. The take-up of business will be very slim compared to leafleting the offices in the high street. You need to think very carefully about any possible promotional efforts which are not traditional adverts.

Used properly, promotional efforts will boost the effects of advertising by helping to make more people aware of your name and by emphasising the benefits of your business in the minds of people who have already seen your adverts. The sorts of additional sales promotion efforts you can choose to establish your initial list of customers include:

- direct mail
- leaflets
- public relations
- exhibition attendance
- canvassing.

You may need some or all of these additional methods depending upon the sort of business you operate and the budget available for promotion.

DIRECT MAIL

Direct mail is the delivery of your advertisements directly to potential customers, without the use of the media. Your advert is delivered, usually by post, right through the letterbox of your likely customers. There are two methods of direct mail — **leafleting** and **selective mailing**.

Leafleting

This is ideal for small businesses operating in a localised area providing services and products for the general public. You can drop leaflets into households if you want to start up a cleaning service, for example, or perhaps if you are manufacturing curtains. By dropping a leaflet into every household in your area you will be sure that *all* your potential customers see the advert, rather than just those who buy the local newspaper.

However, there are some disadvantages to leafleting:

- The time involved in leafleting if you do it yourself.
- The cost of producing many thousands of leaflets.
- Possible public antipathy to advertising material stuffed through the letterbox.

You can reduce these problems if you use the services of an agency or of friends and family for leaflet distribution, and act with courtesy when you deliver.

It's worth investigating the possibility of getting the Post Office to deliver your leaflets. The **Household Delivery Service** can be used by anyone who wants to leaflet every home. The leaflets must not weigh more than 60 grammes, and they must all be identical. The Post Office will want to see a specimen before agreeing to do the distribution. The leaflets must also conform to the British Code of Advertising Practice. A copy of this can be obtained from the Advertising Standards Authority, 2 Torrington Place, London WC1 7HJ. Tel: 020 7580 5555.

Selective mailing

The other form of direct mail involves sending your advertising material to a specific group of people. This is very useful if you want to target a particular group of likely customers. For example, if you are running a business which is aimed at families with children, you would be wasting money by dropping leaflets in every household since not all houses contain children. A better way would be to mail directly to the families you want to see your advertising material — hence the term 'direct mail'.

In order to reach such specific target audiences you need a **mailing list**. These can be bought or rented from various agencies which specialise in producing them. If you want to know more about direct mail contact the British Direct Marketing Association, Haymarket House, 1 Oxendon Street, London SW1Y 4EE. Tel: 020 7321 2525, which can provide you with a list of members who produce mailing lists of every kind. You can of course construct your own mailing list by using *Yellow Pages* and other local directories, like those produced by the various Chambers of Commerce. You can find out about your local chambers from the Association of British Chambers of Commerce, 22 Carlisle Place, London SW1P 1JA. Tel: 020 7565 2000. (www.britishchambers.org.uk).

The main advantage of using selective mailing is:

● the ability to target the most likely customers directly.

The disadvantages are:

● the cost of purchasing mailing lists
● the time consumed in constructing your own mailing list
● the cost of postage.

Writing your own leaflets

Leaflets used in any kind of direct mail campaign can be produced quite cheaply — look in the business pages of broadsheet Sunday newspapers and you will see many advertisements offering to print direct mail leaflets. Without the costs of the artwork you will only be charged around £175 for 1,000 leaflets. The artwork would only cost about £45 making this a highly cost-effective method of reaching your potential customers.

Like advertisements, leaflets need to be eye-catching and they need to sell benefits. Most people do not like the unsolicited mail which lands on the doormat every day so it needs to be highly attractive and heavily geared to benefits selling. For example if you are about to set up a gardening service you could make part of the leaflet a voucher for £20 off the first contract. Your customer will therefore get two benefits:

● a saving of £20
● more time to relax, since you are doing the garden for them.

A headline reading 'relax in your perfect garden and save £20' could attract someone to read your unsolicited leaflet. Simply saying 'Garden

Caring for your pets when you go away on holiday presents you with a number of problems. You need to find someone to care for the animal and then you worry yourself silly during your holiday about whether the pet is being fed or if the house has been burgled because the pet carer has left the door open! The Petcare Hotel can solve both these problems by taking care of your small pet while you go away. There is no other service quite like this.

PET CARE EXPERTISE THAT
RELEASES YOU FROM
HOLIDAY WORRIES

Contact: Angela Petcare
The Petcare Hotel
123 The Way
Smalltown
Largeshire
LG1 2SM
Telephone: Smalltown (0998) 123

Fig. 20. Sample brochure page designs for The Petcare Hotel.

The Petcare Hotel was founded in March 1989 and provides owners of small pets such as gerbils, rabbits and hamsters with someone to look after their animals while on holiday. It provides pet owners with a worry free holiday knowing that their small animal is being cared for by experts in secure surroundings. It is the ideal way to care for pets when you go away.

Fig. 20. Continued.

services now available in Smalltown' will mean the leaflet is likely to wind up in the waste bin.

Apart from the need for a good eye-catching headline your leaflet can contain more words than an advert and it can even include a coupon for people to reply to you. This can be extremely useful since it allows you to build up a mailing list of interested people. Even if they do not do any business with you now, you can lure them with offers in the future.

To write your leaflet, use the benefits and headlines list you used for your advertisements. You can use more than one headline in a leaflet and sell a number of different benefits. However, don't cram your leaflet with facts and figures. All you need is one sheet of A4 paper folded into three printed on both sides. One third will be the front cover which will contain you main eye-catching headline. The inside portions should contain all the other headlines and some explanation of your business. The back of the leaflet can then carry your contact details — look at the example on page 102.

The design and artwork can be done by your local copy shop or commercial printer. Some printers will also handle selective mailings for you, 'stuffing' your leaflets into envelopes and sticking address labels on. Usually, this adds a few pence per item to the postage cost, which you can get discounted if you send more than 5,000 items. If all of these are postcoded you can get a percentage off the total postage price. You can get details of these discounts from your local post office or from the Customer Service Department at your nearest Head Post Office, listed in *Yellow Pages* under Post Office.

PUBLIC RELATIONS

Another method of attracting customers is to launch a **public relations campaign**. This will probably be very much a *press* relations campaign at this stage in your business development. You could write press releases on the launch of your business and mail them to the most appropriate publications. A list of useful publications can be found in the *Willings Press Guide* which can be obtained from your local library or from Hollis Directories, 7 High Street, Teddington TW11 8EL. Tel: 020 8943 3138.

If your press releases are used as the basis for articles you will get editorial coverage of your business which could attract customers to you. Often readers of newspapers and magazines will accept at face value what they read in the editorial columns, but see advertising as biased. In order to increase the chances of an editor using your press release:

● Present it tidily typed in double spacing on one side of the paper only.

● Include at the end of the material all the information which may be needed by the editor, such as your address, telephone number, and availability for interviews.

● Include a professionally taken photograph.

● Include a short background article on you as a person.

A press release should ideally be no more than two sheets of A4 paper — remember that journalists are busy people and will not have time to wade through a short novel giving your life story!

EXHIBITIONS

Another method of attracting customers is by attending an **exhibition**. You can take a stand at an appropriate show and display examples of your products or work. You'll need some posters and some leaflets to hand out. These can be produced by your local copy shop and you can use the headlines you prepared when setting up your first advertisements.

The cost of exhibiting will depend on location, venue and the sort of people attracted to the show. A one-day exhibition in a village hall for the general public is not going to cost as much to take part in as a huge business show at the National Exhibition Centre, for example. Local trade shows will be detailed in your local library's list of events. The nearest Chamber of Commerce will also have information on possible exhibitions. Similarly regional business magazines always carry advertising for possible exhibitors at local shows — check with your Chamber of Commerce for details of the best local business magazines.

A good exhibition stand will have all or most of the following:

● posters
● chairs
● a table
● coffee for your guests
● your product displayed attractively
● leaflets/handouts
● a 'visitors book' so you can compile a mailing list of interested people who visited your stand

PRESS INFORMATION FROM:

The Petcare Hotel, Smalltown

Families with small pets can now rest on holiday knowing that their small animals are being cared for at a brand new hotel.

The Petcare Hotel has just been opened in Smalltown and cares for small pets, such as rabbits, cats, hamsters, mice, budgerigars, and so on, while their owners are away.

According to the owner of the hotel, Miss Angela Petcare: 'Our service will provide pet owners with a worry free break. We can care for their small animals while they are away for the weekend, or even on holiday for a month or two.'

'We have excellent facilities which are open to inspection so that a pet owner can check them out in advance of sending their animal to use for a week or two.'

The Petcare Hotel has been approved by the veterinary surgeons at The High Street, Smalltown, who will provide a backup service for any animals which fall ill during their stay. The Proprietor, Miss Petcare, is a former veterinary receptionist, and has been especially trained in dealing with small pets. The new hotel already has a number of residents, including six gerbils, three mice and two rabbits! The average cost of the use of the hotel is only £18 per week.

'I think this is excellent value,' said Miss Petcare. 'It will relieve pet owners of any worry when they are on holiday. They will be able to relax knowing that their pet is being well looked after.'

Unlike 'kennels', The Petcare Hotel will only care for small animals, and will not keep larger species such as dogs.

For further information contact:

Angela Petcare   Tel. (0998) 123
The Petcare Hotel
123 The Way
Smalltown
Largeshire LG1 2SM

Notes for editors

Angela Petcare is available for interview. Please call for an appointment. Photographers may attend at 9am on 18th January 1999 when the hotel's first armadillo will be taking up residence for a fortnight.

Fig. 21. A sample press release: clear, concise and to the point.

- small promotional items — perhaps something connected with your product or service, inscribed with your name and phone number.

Exhibitions can be very useful ways of establishing links with potential customers. However, they can be a waste of time if you have not planned carefully in advance, so:

- make sure that this exhibition will attract the kind of customer you want
- have plenty of business cards available and pens that work
- make sure your leaflets/handouts won't run out
- keep the coffee hot and readily available
- be prepared for a long, exhausting day — possibly 10am to 8pm with no break, in smart clothes, probably in a hot stuffy atmosphere.

Going off to 'do a show' may sound fun but it's incredibly hard work!

CANVASSING

Another method of getting your first customers is by canvassing. This can either be done on a door-to-door basis, or by telephoning the sorts of people and businesses who might be potential customers. Be prepared for a lot of people who are simply not interested and some who may even be downright rude! You must have a thick skin for this method of attracting customers, but it obviously works as many established companies use it. As with other sorts of promotion it can be a sort of 'numbers game'. For example, after a few weeks you could discover that every 100 calls lead to 3.5 enquiries and 1.2 firm sales. Such information helps you plan more effectively.

SUMMARY

The most common ways to attract customers are:

- advertising
- direct mail
- internet sites
- public relations
- exhibitions
- canvassing.

You will probably use a combination of some or all of these methods in your first attempts to get customers, so make sure that your plan is co-ordinated. For instance, make sure that you send a press release out so that the material can be used in the same week as you advertise. This will have a double impact: if your press release arrives after your adverts appear it is no longer a news story, so you will not get any editorial coverage. If your press release goes out too soon, the readers will have forgotten all about you by the time your advert appears!

Once you have developed your basic ideas for marketing your business, and decided where and when you will advertise, to whom you will send press releases, and to what extent you will get involved in direct mail, remember to write it down and keep records of all of this information on file!

At the beginning of this chapter we saw that the first part of your marketing plan is identifying the objectives you want to achieve. The rest of the plan will be a combination of advertising, direct mail, and so on to help you achieve your twofold aim of attracting and keeping customers. The reason you need to write down the marketing plan is so that you can monitor its success. If you know exactly how much direct mail you sent, and to whom, you will be able to calculate the effect of that part of your scheme when your customers start coming in.

CHECKLIST

● Write down your marketing plan, with the initial aim of attracting new customers.

● Choose the correct medium for your business — or perhaps a combination of several media.

● Always check the value-for-money which you are getting for your publicity — for example, how many people are you reaching per pound spent?

● If absolutely necessary, hire professionals to write or design adverts — bad publicity will probably be worse than no publicity at all.

● Always budget for publicity in your cash flow forecasts. If you overspend, rewrite your forecast accordingly.

7

Keeping Customers

Once you have attracted your initial set of customers, you need to make sure that they repeat their orders and come back for more work. One of the most important aspects of keeping customers is **pricing** your goods and services competitively — so important, in fact, that the next chapter is entirely devoted to it. Suffice to say you must price your goods or services properly if you are to maintain a list of clients who come back for more. If your prices are too high you will not get repeat business. Similarly, if your prices are too low your customers will wonder what corners you are cutting.

The other main aspects of keeping your customers are **image** and **customer service**.

CREATING THE RIGHT IMAGE

If you provide quotations for customers on a scrap of paper, you will not fare well against competitors who use properly printed quotation forms. If you turn up to see a client dressed in tatty clothing, you will not be recommended to others. Image is vital in business; indeed large corporations spend millions on getting it just right. You too should spend time, and some money, on ensuring that your business has the **right image**.

Stationery
Your business image begins with how you present yourself on paper, and professionally produced **stationery** is a must. Local copy shops are good places to go for this work. The staff will be able to advise on design, typefaces and quality of paper. Here, though are a few rules.

- Use good quality paper.
- Colour of paper — white is preferable. If you must have a colour choose grey or cream. Bright colours *will not* catch the attention of your customers, and can be hard to photocopy.
- Choose a bold, solid typeface which is easy to read.
- Avoid the use of pretty pictures.
- Avoid fancy borders, rules, and so on.

Once you have decided on your stationery think about the information you want printed on it. You will need the following:

- your business name, plus your own name if it is not the same as that of the business
- full address including postcode
- telephone number including STD code
- other contact points, such as telex or facsimile numbers
- an indication of the type of business carried out (e.g. 'Plumber', 'Public Relations consultant', Business Services') which briefly describes the sort of work you will perform

Use the same quality of paper, the same type style, and basic design on all other items of stationery. The usual stationery you will require will be:

- paper for correspondence
- business cards
- compliments slips.

In addition, you may want to print duplicate invoice sets, order forms, and other kinds of stationery specific to your needs, but you could use your correspondence paper for these, simply type in the word 'invoice', for example, at the top of the page. If you do use your headed notepaper for invoices you will need to add your VAT registration number, if applicable. Indeed, if you are VAT registered your VAT number *must* appear on all your invoices.

In the case of a limited company, you should also include the registration number of that company and the names of the directors on your headed notepaper, invoices, orders and quotations.

Pre-printed stationery

You can now buy pre-printed stationery for letterheads, business cards and so on. The items are printed in colour and can be used in your computer printer. In this way you can have the professional look of cleverly designed stationery without having to pay the full design costs. You can get such stationery from most good stationers. Or you can get it via mail order, from one of the main suppliers Paper Direct. To order their latest catalogue call 0800 616244.

Writing letters

Once you have your stationery make sure that you use it to the best effect. Your correspondence should be:

**Holidays in Style
for Your Small Pet**

The Petcare Hotel
123 The Way
Smalltown
Largeshire
LG1 2SM

Telephone: Smalltown (0998) 123

_____

Proprietor: Miss Angela Petcare
VAT Registration No: 000 0000 00

Fig. 22. Simple but smart printed stationery will help to improve
the image of your business.

Fig. 23. Formats for business correspondence — letters can be
set out in any one of these ways.

- attractively laid out — don't bunch all the type at the top of the page, for instance
- grammatically correct
- direct and to the point
- free of spelling mistakes
- properly addressed.

Letters which do not conform to these rules will harm your image, and may put off potential customers. If you do not know enough grammar, or cannot spell, the following books would be useful:

- a good dictionary, such as *Chambers*
- a guide to grammar, such as *Oxford English* (Oxford)
- a guide to punctuation such as *Mind the Stop* (Penguin).

Some typical business letters are shown on the opposite page.

Your telephone manner

The next major contributor to your business image is the way in which you handle the **telephone**. Follow these rules to improve your telephone image:

- Always answer the telephone with your own name, company name or the exchange and the number (eg Smalltown 123). This confirms to the caller that they have been connected to the right number, and is also more professional than a blunt ''Ello' or an even shorter 'Yeh'.

- When calling someone always give your name, and your business name if it is different, at the start of the conversation. There is nothing so infuriating as listening to someone talk on the telephone without knowing who they are.

- Always explain your reason for calling at the beginning of the conversation.

- Always try to be helpful to callers. If your business cannot provide them with the sort of things they want, try to suggest names of people who might. This adds to your image.

- If you have an answerphone, make sure that your recorded message is clear and concise and that you always respond to messages.

Telephoning

Some things to say

Can I help you?	It's a pleasure.
How can I help you?	Thank you for calling.
May we be of service?	Thank you for being so
May I take your name	helpful.
and address?	Thank you very much for
May I call you back later?	letting us quote.
How can we assist you?	Good morning.

Some things not to say

Who? No, he's out.	It's not my fault.
Don't know when she'll be	What about the month after
back.	next?
Sorry, couldn't say.	It's no use blaming me.
Sorry mate, haven't the	No-one told us.
foggiest.	Same to you.
You want someone else.	

One final point about telephone manners — if your business is using the same line as your residence, make sure your family know how to be polite and helpful, and will take messages accurately. Nothing could be worse for your business than an important client trying to deal with an awkward teenager instead of you!

Personal appearance

The way you dress and the way you behave are important aspects of your business image. No-one will expect a window-cleaner to wear a three-piece suit, but they will expect that you are reasonably presented and that you don't have hair that hasn't been washed for a fortnight or fingernails that are black with grime. They will also expect you to have some sense of diplomacy since you'll probably see things in your customers' windows that they would rather you didn't! If you are dirty, scruffy and tactless you will not get repeat business.

Similarly, customers will expect a management consultant to turn up neatly dressed, clean and tidy. Your hair will need to be well kept and your breath must be fresh as you will be in close contact with your customers. All this sort of advice may sound patronising and obvious. But it is amazing how many people in business present themselves poorly. If you smarten up your own personal image you'll get the repeat orders that the competition doesn't.

PROVIDING CUSTOMER SERVICE

Customer service is an all-embracing term which covers those added extras which are not part of the actual product or service you are selling. Efficiency, on-time delivery, and cost-effectiveness are some of the main components of customer service. It is particularly important that a job is completed on time. Late delivery or completion is one of the most frequent causes of customers' complaints. Try to think of things which will help your customers. The more help you provide which is not asked for, or charged for, the more likely you are to receive continued support and repeat orders. Customers are also likely to recommend your business to others — a very valuable means of attracting new custom. Do not underestimate the value of 'word of mouth' advertising!

The sort of added extras you can provide as part of a customer service package will depend on the sort of business you operate, but here are some ideas to consider:

- free delivery
- free telephone advice on use of product in the six weeks after purchase
- free training in use of product
- extended guarantee of product for nominal fee
- low price maintenance contract
- reduced prices on further orders in the six months after first purchase
- six items for the price of five.

Your customer service plan

Many companies now issue a **statement of customer service**. If you can produce your own customer service plan you will be sure to attract repeat orders since your purchasers know that they will benefit from your additional efforts — you're providing much more than just a product or service. They will also tell their friends and contacts about your added extras, which will help bring in new customers. A customer service plan could be a vital document for your business.

Writing your plan

Begin your plan by writing down those items of customer service that you wish to provide, using the list above for inspiration if necessary.

CUSTOMER SERVICE PLAN

1. FREE collection of all pets staying for one week or more

2. FREE return of pets to their homes after stay of one week or more

3. 10% DISCOUNT for pets who are booked in for four weeks or more during 12 months

4. FREE telephone advice on pet care to all customers

Fig. 24. The sort of customer service plan which the Petcare Hotel might be able to offer.

Next, decide the order in which they would appeal to your potential customers. This will depend upon the sort of business you are offering. For example, if you're selling home-grown vegetables, free delivery may be a very attractive item of customer service. However, if you provided a service your customer would be much more interested in the possibility of discounts on future contracts with you. Of course, discounts would also appeal to people buying lots of vegetables, like hotels and restaurants, so this could be an item in the first customer service plan as well. But it would be less appealing than free delivery since that would apply to more customers. So, sort out the items of customer service you intend to supply so that they are in order of priority in your list.

You can now use this list to produce a small leaflet or card to give to all customers and potential clients. An example of a customer service plan is shown above.

Offering guarantees

Another means of improving your customer service is to provide **guarantees**. Usually guarantees are only of real benefit to people who supply products although some services can have a form of guarantee provided for them. If you make tables, for example, you could guarantee that the surface is heat resistant. Alternatively, if you offer secretarial services you could guarantee that all work is completed within four hours of receipt. But remember — make sure you can back these guarantees. If your guarantees aren't substantiated, you can be sued.

Providing a guarantee on a product or service implies that you will correct any defects should they occur. It also implies that these defects

GUARANTEE

1. The Petcare Hotel GUARANTEES to keep all pets indoors overnight in centrally heated accommodation. All pets will be fed twice daily and all cages will be cleaned at least twice each week. Daily exercise will be provided for all of the larger animals which attend the Petcare Hotel.

2. The Petcare Hotel also GUARANTEES to provide immediate veterinary attention for any animal which develops an illness during its stay.

3. The Petcare Hotel GUARANTEES that all payments will be refunded in the event of any animal dying during its stay at the hotel and whose death has been caused by the Hotel.

Fig. 25. A sample guarantee for the Petcare Hotel.

will not occur! If your products or services fail to meet their guaranteed status you are liable to correct the problem, so don't make guarantees you cannot keep. However, your customers will expect some form of guarantee from you even if it is not provided in writing. They may want you to guarantee that you will supply the goods by a certain date, for example. If you agree to such terms your guarantee will form part of your contract and if you do not perform the requested task you will be in breach of contract.

If you can support your products with a rock solid guarantee, such as the one above, put it in writing and give your customers and potential customers a copy of the guarantee. This helps increase your professional image and boosts the confidence of the purchaser in your products or services. The fact that you agree to repair or replace any faults mentioned in your guarantee means that your level of customer service is higher than your competitors who do not offer guarantees and so you increase your chances of keeping customers. Offering guarantees that are kept will mean that your customers are prepared to pass on your name to others — the ever-important word of mouth advertising again.

OTHER METHODS OF KEEPING CUSTOMERS

Creating and maintaining a good image and supporting it with a high level of customer service is not the only way to keep your customers and stop them from going to the competition. Investigate every possible way of keeping your clients.

Business gifts

Business gifts are an accepted way of keeping in good favour with customers. Christmas is the usual time to give small presents to your valued customers, although you can use any excuse such as the anniversary of your business start-up.

If possible, try to have your name and address printed on the gifts. This helps promote your business since many business gifts, such as jotters or desk sets, will be on permanent display — and so act as a free advertisement.

Business gifts are advertised in magazines such as *Marketing Week* and *Campaign*. They are also advertised in *Exchange and Mart* as well as various executive magazines, such as those distributed free by the various charge card companies or airlines. One excellent source of business gifts which can be overprinted with your name is Promark Business Gifts. Tel: (01491) 671539. They sell everything from pens and pencils to mugs, place mats, leather executive cases, diaries, calculators, cut glass and even overprinted golf balls!

Also remember to mail Christmas cards to your customers each year and you could even send the important ones postcards from your holiday. Such items show that you care about the customer and that makes them feel wanted.

Keeping in touch

Another good idea is keeping your customers in touch with your activities. If you only ever speak to a customer when they order goods or services from you, you will convey the impression that all you want is their money. Whilst this may well be true, you will get more of their money if you make them believe this is not all you want! Make your customers feel as though they are your friends — indeed your good customers may well become good friends.

Don't be afraid to keep in touch with customers even if they are not actually buying something from you. If you haven't heard from a particular customer for a while, call them to find out how they are and to remind them gently that you still sell items they might require! If you adopt a time management system (see Chapter 10) make a note to call customers at a specific time in the future after their last business dealing with you. If you are in touch in the meantime, just put the date for the call back. Thus you will always have a reminder to call your customers if they haven't been in touch with you. As a result they will feel much more wanted.

Customer updates

You can also make customers feel part of your community by supplying them with regular updates on your business activities. Some large firms have their own newspapers or magazines which they send to their clients. Self-employed people can also benefit from this idea by writing their own small newsletter or just a long letter which is then mailed to their customers. People do not like feeling that they are merely lining your pockets, so making them feel part of your circle of friends and contacts will make sure that they think of you before they think of the competition.

Parties

Another way of making your customers feel wanted is to have a **party**. Many companies have Christmas parties or New Year celebrations — how about arranging a similar function for your own customers? If you have a garden why not hold a summer barbecue? They will appreciate the invitation and you will not compete with the endless round of lunches and receptions which occur in December. You can also organise other social events such as trips to the theatre. Obviously, this will cost you and you must budget for it in your cash flow forecasts but if you *can* afford some kind of social event — even if it is just a pleasant lunch — you will certainly benefit from the increased respect you gain from your customers.

Perhaps this all sounds a bit too much for your particular business. Lunches and trips to the theatre may sound fine for people offering management consultancy, you may think, but not for a car washer! But you would be wrong. Even this sort of business could benefit from a social gathering for its customers. Say, for example, you organised a car treasure hunt for customers in a certain town. The 'treasure' is actually a barbecue at your house and all of the clues lead to your address. Your customers will arrive, enjoy some drinks and a meal at your expense and have a thoroughly good time which was made more fun by the intrigue of the treasure hunt. The prize for the first person to find the treasure could be a voucher for free car cleaning for three months. The social event would cost some money but may well bring better results than a simple advertisement costing just as much.

Other ideas for keeping customers

- Form a 'club' of your best customers who get special deals on your products and services.

- Pass on your customers' business details to other clients of yours who may need their services. In this way you form a 'network' of businesses.

● Plan to improve and upgrade your products and services on a regular basis so that customers are tempted to buy again and again.

The golden rule

However, even if you follow all these tips and ideas for maintaining your customer base and getting repeat orders nothing, absolutely nothing will replace the following advice:

● **Provide your customers with the right product, at the right time, and at the right price.**

The right price is discussed in the next chapter; doing the work on time is up to you.

CHECKLIST

● Maintain a good personal image.
● Have a good image on paper.
● Use the telephone properly and courteously.
● Develop a customer service plan.
● Provide guarantees that you will stick to.
● Make your customers feel wanted.
● Do all your work accurately and on time.

8

Pricing

Fixing a price for your products or services can be difficult. You don't want to charge too much in case you put people off buying from you, and you don't want to charge too little as they may wonder what corners you are cutting to achieve such low price levels!

If you have done your planning properly, and obtained extensive information on your competitors, you will know how much they charge, and so will be able to fix a similar price. However, do set a price which is specifically geared to providing you with a **profit** — calculate how many hours it takes to do each job, the amount of money it costs you per hour to produce the work, and the amount of profit you want to make.

CALCULATING YOUR PRICES

Your hourly rate to break even

Use the format on page 122 to calculate your hourly rate. Then multiply this by the number of hours it will take to complete each job. This will provide you with the charge you must make merely to **break even**. You should then add to this the profit you wish to make. Recalculate the hourly rate every six months so that you can increase prices if necessary. This format assumes that you are the sole earner. If your home has more than one income you should apportion items like rent, mortgage, rates, etc, so that the amount included reflects the extent of the contribution you will have to make. Enter monthly costs. At this stage you may need to estimate some items, such as postage, stationery and raw materials, as they will fluctuate according to the amount of work you have. Once your workload is more settled, say in two or three months, recalculate the hourly rate so that you can check the pricing.

This total provides you with the monthly income you need to cover your outgoings. To find your hourly rate divide this total by the number of hours you will work each month. Don't over-estimate your hours. Although you will probably work long hours, especially in the early stages of setting up your business, don't overwork — tiredness reduces efficiency. A working week for most people at home should be around

Monthly outgoings

Accountancy fees	£	_____
Advertising	£	_____
Bank charges	£	_____
Books/magazines for business use	£	_____
Car tax	£	_____
Depreciation of equipment	£	_____
Entertainment of clients	£	_____
Equipment hire charge	£	_____
Fuel bill	£	_____
Insurance premiums	£	_____
Internet costs	£	_____
Loan repayments	£	_____
Miscellaneous expenses	£	_____
Mortgage/rent	£	_____
National Insurance	£	_____
Pension premiums	£	_____
Petrol (business use)	£	_____
Postage	£	_____
Rates	£	_____
Raw materials	£	_____
Stationery	£	_____
Tax	£	_____
Telephone bills (including mobile)	£	_____
Travel expenses	£	_____
Other items	£	_____
TOTAL PER MONTH (200 hours)	£	_____
TOTAL PER HOUR	£	_____

Fig. 26. Budget of outgoings per month/per hour.

50 hours. On that basis, divide the monthly total in the price calculator table by 200.

You now have your hourly break-even charge — the amount you will need to charge if you are to pay all your business bills and provide yourself with a roof over your head. However, you would not have any personal income if you simply charged this amount. You wouldn't be able to buy clothes, have the house decorated, or go out to dinner. All of these items need to come from your profits, so now you need to calculate the amount of **personal** income you want to get from your business. The list below will help you analyse the amount of profit you want. Again, enter expenses on a monthly basis.

Your personal income requirements

Bank charges	£ _____
Car tax	£ _____
Clothes	£ _____
Entertaining	£ _____
Food etc	£ _____
Gifts	£ _____
Hobbies	£ _____
Holidays	£ _____
Household spending (decorating etc)	£ _____
Miscellaneous expenses	£ _____
Newspapers/magazines/books	£ _____
Personal gifts	£ _____
Personal telephone charges	£ _____
Pet care	£ _____
Schooling	£ _____
Sports	£ _____
Television licence	£ _____
Toys etc	£ _____
Travel	£ _____
Other items	£ _____
TOTAL PER MONTH (200 hours)	£ _____
TOTAL PER HOUR	£ _____

Fig. 27. Calculating your personal income requirements.

This total provides you with the monthly amount of personal income needed. It does not include any savings or emergency cash. As before, divide this amount by 200 to find the hourly rate.

Contingencies

In addition to this amount estimate the extra cash you want available for **emergencies,** how much you want to **save,** and how much you want available in order to **expand** your business. Having decided upon these figures, work out their hourly rates — divide the annual cash you want in hand by 2,400 (the estimated number of hours you will work per year) — then complete the table below (figure 28).

Hourly charge required

Break-even business costs per hour   £ _____

Personal income per hour   £ _____

Emergency fund per hour   £ _____

Savings per hour   £ _____

Money for business expansion per hour   £ _____

GRAND TOTAL TO CHARGE PER HOUR £ _____

Fig. 28. Calculating your hourly charge.

This grand total now shows the amount of money you need to charge per hour to satisfy all your financial needs. However, it is wise to err on the side of caution, so add a further 10% to cope with any unexpected problems. You now have your hourly fee, which you can use to calculate the cost of any particular job.

Of course to calculate your price in this way, you need to know a number of things which might be unknown quantities when you begin business, for example:

●   how long each particular job will take
●   all your financial requirements for the best part of a year.

However, if at all possible, do try to charge your work according to the time it takes. For example, perhaps you manufacture wooden egg cups and it takes around five minutes to produce each item. You know that you need £18 per hour to cover all your financial needs, so for ten cups an hour you would need to charge £1.80 per product. If you were to charge only £1.50 per cup, the 'fair price' you think people would pay, your business would have to lower your prices and seek ways of reducing your hourly costs.

Using your account

Having a proper set of accounts (see Chapter 9) is a vital tool in pricing as it enables you to see exactly where your money is going and so helps you to change your spending and keep costs down. So although it is best to price your goods and services based upon your hourly financial needs, you must be flexible and use your accounts to make sure that your costs do not get out of hand. If they become too steep, you will have to increase the price of your products or service. This could make your prices unattractive compared to the competition and you could lose customers. So the moral is — keep a firm grip on your business finances if you want to profit from your endeavours.

MANAGING YOUR PRICE LEVELS

Price increases

Naturally, you'll have to increase your prices occasionally to make sure that your profits remain constant. Try not to increase your prices more than once a year, as this will annoy your customers and make them look more seriously at the competition. However, price changes in the early days of your business will be tolerated as long as they are fully justified.

To work out price increases, simply repeat the above process, taking into account any increases in your hourly financial needs. Your costs will inevitably rise over a year's trading and you will need to pass those increases on to your customers if your profits are not to dwindle — but always check your competitors' current charges before raising your own. If you become more expensive without providing extra customer service you will lose business. However, if your hourly financial requirement needs the higher fees, you'll have to compromise by lowering the proposed increase and reducing your spending.

Follow through

When you have finally decided on a new price be sure to let your customers know about the increase. Write a letter to all your existing clients, or add something in your customer newsletter if you publish one. Also remember to update your sales literature and your advertisements. If you are not registered for VAT you must check whether your price increase will bring you within the VAT registration limits. If it does, apply immediately. You must also recalculate your cash flow forecast for the following year so that you know exactly how your business will fare with your new pricing structure. Putting up your prices is not simply a matter of adding 10% because you'd like a bit of extra cash!

Discounts

Many companies offer discounts and your business may benefit from such a scheme. However, don't give discounts to anyone and everyone.

Holidays in Style
for Your Small Pet

The Petcare Hotel
123 The Way
Smalltown
Largeshire
LG1 2SM

Telephone: Smalltown (0998) 123

QUOTATION No: Q37	DATE: 5th July 199X

Mr and Mrs Dogowner 3 The Cuttings Smalltown Largeshire	CUSTOMER No: 88

Item	Item Price	Total
To care for two baby gerbils for two weeks Provide accommodation and all standard foodstuffs	17.00	68.00
Special dietary requirements for one gerbil	4.50	4.50
Your attention is drawn to the Terms of Trading attached, particularly Clause 4		
Payment will be due within 30 days of the presentation of the invoice		
VAT is not applicable		
TOTAL ESTIMATED FEE		£72.50

Proprietor: Miss Angela Petcare

Fig. 29. A specially printed quotation form.

Holidays in Style
for Your Small Pet

The Petcare Hotel
123 The Way
Smalltown
Largeshire
LG1 2SM

Telephone: Smalltown (0998) 123

QUOTATION

Mr and Mrs Dogowner
3 The Cuttings
Smalltown
Largeshire

5th July 199X

TO:

Caring for Sooty, a male cat, for three weeks £66

This fee includes all accommodation and food charges, but excludes any necessary veterinary bills. Transportation to and from The Petcare Hotel is at the owner's expense.

Value Added Tax is applicable to all charges and will be at the rate in force at the time of invoicing (Currently 17½%).

TERM: Payment due within 30 days. Cheques should be made payable to The Petcare Hotel. A 5% discount is available for payment in advance.

QUOTATION No: 5678

Proprietor: Miss Angela Petcare
VAT Registrtation No: 000 0000 00

Fig. 30. A quotation laid out more simply on headed notepaper.

They must also bring in some advantage to your business. If you get nothing in return from a discount you are effectively giving your customers money. That will eat into your profits and do your business no good at all.

Discounts can be offered to certain customers for a number of reasons. For example, you could offer discounts for payment with order. This means that you do not need to offer credit. If you provide a product or service, then invoice the customer some weeks later, to receive payment up to 30 days after the invoice, the customer is effectively borrowing money from you every day that he has both your product and his money in his hands. That is a real cost which can be avoided if people pay up with their orders. However, you have to make that option more attractive to them than the free credit you give for a month or so. A small discount may be all that is needed to make them pay up. This provides immediate funds to your business and reduces the costs incurred by offering credit terms.

Another reason for discounts could be for customers who buy more than a specified number of items. Bulk buying discounts encourage customers to buy larger amounts of goods to reduce the unit cost. This increases your volume of business and so adds to your profits. However, do not set the bulk discount level so low that everyone qualifies — you will only lower your overall income. The discount level should be just low enough to encourage a fair proportion of your customers to make larger orders — and so increase your overall income.

Sales

Holding a sale is another means of generating business and controlling price. If you hold a sale it will encourage your competitors to keep their prices down. If that occurs the whole market is stimulated and more customers are generated for all of you. At the same time sales stimulate more interest in your own business and also allow you to sell off old stock before putting your prices up. Holding a sale for a service-based business is not always possible, but it may stimulate more custom and is a useful promotional gimmick if nothing else.

Publicising your prices

Your potential customers will always want to know your prices, so publish a detailed price list if possible. Nothing puts customers off buying something more than not knowing the price. Without a price, potential customers will think your product or service is too expensive. Be honest about your prices. It is a vital factor in the customers' decision whether or not to purchase and you must therefore tell them.

If you sell products or a standardised range of services you can produce a price list. However, if you offer a service which is different for each client you cannot calculate a standard price. You will therefore have to produce a detailed quotation for each job, such as those on pages 126 and 127.

Your quotation is part of the contract between you and your customer, so make sure it is accurate and leaves no room for misinterpretation. If you provide a written quotation like this you cannot change the price later without your customer's consent. Having said this, written quotations will help create a professional image for your business, and so are probably worthwhile. Make sure that your quotations are only valid for a few weeks, a month at the most; then you can change the price if the purchase is made at a later date when your costs have gone up.

The price rule

However you let your customers know about your prices, there is one rule to remember:

● **Charge the maximum price your customers are prepared to pay and get them to pay quickly.**

To follow this rule, you need to know:

(a) the prices of the competition
(b) your costs and profit requirements.

Use these two factors to calculate your price — if the customers are prepared to pay, all well and good. If they begin to grumble, check your costs again and see if you can reduce them, so that you can lower your prices without damaging your profits.

CHECKLIST

To make sure that you charge the right price:

● Check what the competition charges and price your goods at around the same level.
● Work out your costs on an hourly basis so you know how much you need to charge for each hour's work or for the number of products manufactured per hour.
● Offer genuine discounts to certain customers.
● Hold sales prior to price increases to stimulate the market.
● Always publish price lists.
● Produce written quotations.

9

Keeping Accounts

If your business is to be well run, and you are to satisfy the authorities that you are paying the right amount of tax and VAT, you will need to keep accurate *and* up-to-date **accounts**. Before you start any kind of accounts, check with your accountant that you will be doing the **book-keeping** on a basis which suits him or her.

INVOICING

Invoicing is the first part of your accounting process. You cannot keep any accounts unless you get some money in! Invoicing is a vital aspect of accounting and must be done properly.

Your invoices should preferably use the same layout, typeface, paper and so on as your headed notepaper. You can buy books of invoices, but they do not look as professional as printed headed invoices. If you are VAT registered you must print your VAT number on the stationery as well as all the other basic details of your business. You could either use your headed notepaper and simply type 'invoice' at the top, or you could have pre-printed invoices specially prepared. You might consider this an unnecessary expense, but it does help your image, especially if your customers are big businesses.

Your invoices should contain the following information:

- your business name, and your own name if it is not the same as that of the business
- your address, including postcode
- your telephone number, including STD code
- any other numbers such as fax or internet address
- the name and address of the person being invoiced
- details of what the invoice is for
- the price to be paid
- any discounts which apply
- the terms of payment.

VAT invoices ('tax invoices')

If you are **VAT registered** you are required to show the following additional information on your invoices:

● your VAT registration number
● a number which identifies the particular invoice
● the date of the invoice
● the 'tax point' (this is the date at which the VAT is applied to the price. In most instances this will also be the date of the invoice, but there are exceptions which are listed in the documentation you receive from HM Customs and Excise when you register as a VAT trader.)
● the VAT rate on each item
● the amount of VAT on each item
● the total amount of VAT which is due
● the total amount excluding VAT
● the rate of any discounts applied
● a full description of the items charged for on the invoice
● a description of the type of supply, eg sales, hire purchase, loan, and so on.

A VAT invoice is known officially as a **tax invoice**. Less detailed tax invoices are allowable for certain traders, such as retailers. You can get full details of the sort of invoice you should issue from your local HM Customs and Excise department, and from your accountant. If in doubt, it is best to issue the full tax invoices which contain all the information listed above.

BOOK-KEEPING

The main administrative task is to keep accurate and up-to-date books. You will need accounting books to record:

● sales made
● purchases made using cheques
● purchases made with petty cash
● purchases made with credit cards — if you use the VAT cash accounting scheme.

You will also need two extra books for VAT summaries, if you are VAT registered.

Holidays in Style
for Your Small Pet

The Petcare Hotel
123 The Way
Smalltown
Largeshire
LG1 2SM

Telephone: Smalltown (0998) 123

INVOICE No: 8000	DATE: 12th July 199X

Mr and Mrs Dogowner
3 The Cuttings
Smalltown
Largeshire

CUSTOMER No: 88

Item	Item Price	Total
Caring for two baby gerbils for two weeks	17.00	68.00
Special dietary requirements for one gerbil	4.50	4.50
TERMS: Payment due within 30 days. See also 'Terms of Trading'		
TOTAL		£72.50

Proprietor: Miss Angela Petcare

Fig. 31. A specially printed invoice form.
It may be worthwhile for your business to have invoices specially
printed, perhaps with a similar layout to this one.

Holidays in Style
for Your Small Pet

The Petcare Hotel
123 The Way
Smalltown
Largeshire
LG1 2SM

Telephone: Smalltown (0998) 123

INVOICE

Dear Mr and Mrs Dogowner
3 The Cuttings
Smalltown
Largeshire

12th July 199X

TO:

Caring for Sooty, a male cat, for three weeks	£66.00
Value Added Tax at 17½%	£11.55
TOTAL	£77.55

TERMS: Payment due within 30 days

INVOICE No: 1234

Tax Point: 12/7/9X

Proprietor: Miss Angela Petcare
VAT Registration No: 000 0000 00

Fig. 32. An invoice typed on headed notepaper.
This particular example is a VAT or tax invoice.

Sales book

Your **sales book** will record details of all the invoices you have issued and the dates when those invoices have been paid so that you can keep a check on your income. Record the following data in your sales book:

- invoice date
- invoice number
- person/company to whom invoice was issued
- amount due
- date invoice paid.

If you are VAT registered you will need two further columns:

1. VAT due
2. gross amount due of total fees plus the VAT.

Completing the sales book is simple: just transfer the information on your invoices into the relevant columns. It's best to separate the material into monthly segments so that you can analyse your income accurately. You will need to know, for example, if every January is going to be a bad month, or if every August is going to be so busy you will need to buy extra raw materials. If the figures are jumbled up it will be more difficult to find management information like this.

Bank payments and deposits book (cash book)

This book will record all the money paid into your **bank account** as well as all the **purchases** made by cheque. You will need columns for the following information:

- date
- total amount paid into the bank
- amount paid in from sales
- VAT paid in from sales
- amount paid in from other sources
- amount paid out from bank
- cheque number
- receipt number
- VAT paid (if you are VAT registered)
- person/company to whom the cheque was made out
- analysis of payment (eg petrol, office supplies).

You will need to analyse your payments by using **double-entry**

book-keeping. Basically this means that you enter the amount you pay with each cheque into two columns — one representing all payments made from your bank account, and the other for the specific supply to which that payment relates, such as stationery or petrol. You will need a number of columns depending on the analysis you want to make. The following is a representative list:

- books/magazines/journals etc
- insurance premiums
- office equipment
- petrol
- professional subscriptions
- raw materials
- stationery
- telephone charges
- travel
- others.

If you are VAT registered, a column is needed for VAT. The analysis of all your payments will enable you to keep track of your spending on particular items.

It is a good idea to have a column for 'other items', which is used to record those occasional payments which do not merit their own column. These might include bank charges and other monthly or quarterly payments.

Drawings

You should also have a column for **drawings**. Drawings are the monies you extract from your business for your personal use. Self-employed people can take as much money out of their business as they want — you are taxed on your *total profits*, which will of course include the money you use personally. There is nothing to stop you using all your profits for personal use, but this would be dangerous for your business, as there would not be any resources for further development, or for times of trouble in the future. Try to limit your drawings to the amount you actually need, leaving the remaining income for reinvestment in the business. This will also help reduce your tax bill, since you will gain tax relief on any money spent on equipment or other items used in the business. Expanding your business is therefore an excellent way of keeping your tax bill down!

If you run a limited company, you will not have drawings as such because you will pay yourself a salary. The difference is that a salary is

	Sales Book				
DATE	CUSTOMER	INVOICE No	AMOUNT	AMOUNT PAID	DATE PAID
3/4	Smith	8801	175.00	175.00	3/4
4/4	Brown	8802	225.00	225.00	4/4
5/4	Jones	8803	300.00		
8/4	Wright	8804	100.00	100.00	12/4
10/4	Wong	8805	125.00	125.00	10/4
18/4	Green	8806	100.00	50.00	22/4
22/4	White	8807	275.00		
23/4	Smythe	8808	325.00	325.00	30/4
TOTALS FOR MONTH			1,625.00	1000.00	

Fig. 33. A sample page from a sales book.

INCOME   **EXPENDITURE**

DATE	PAID IN TO BANK	SALES	VAT	OTHER	PAYEE	RCPT No	CHEQUE No	AMOUNT	VAT	PETROL	OFFICE SUPPLIES	DRAWINGS	OTHER ITEMS
5/1	250.00	212.77	37.23		Garage	84	01234	10.20	1.52	8.68			
7/1	172.50	146.81	25.69										
12/1					Garage	85	01235	11.50	1.71	9.79			
13/1	1,250.00	851.06	148.94	250.00 (Refund from bank after error)	Stationers	86	01236	84.90	12.65		72.31		
15/1	150.00	127.66	22.34										
18/1					Self	87	01237	110.80				110.80	
22/1					Stationers	88	01238	32.20	4.80		27.40		
25/1					Bookshop	89	01239	15.00					15.00 (Ref. Books)
28/1					Garage			15.70	2.34	13.36			
Totals	1,822.50	1338.30	234.20	250.00				280.30	23.02	31.83	99.71	110.80	15.00

Fig. 34. The bank payments and deposit book ('cash book') will help you keep a close eye on the amount of money in your account.

normally a regular payment. Drawings can be any amount, drawn at any time.

Receipts

Another analysis column you must include is 'receipt number'. Every time you make a payment from your cheque book you should ask for a receipt. These receipts should then be numbered and stored in a file, and the number also written on the cheque stub to which it applies. In this way, the tax authorities will be able to check that you are spending money in the way you claim. It's a wise precaution because if you do not get receipts and store them properly, you could find it difficult claiming tax relief in some instances.

Summary

Your bank payments and deposits book should:

- show every item paid into your bank account
- show every payment made from your bank account (including standing orders and direct debits)
- be updated at least once a week, if not daily
- cross reference every payment to a receipt number and cheque number
- show all the VAT received and paid in each month.

Petty cash book

The other main accounts book you will need is to record the payments you make into and from your **petty cash** tin. Some payments such as for newspapers or stamps will not need a cheque, and will be made in cash, but you still need to account for them properly. The petty cash book will need to show the following information:

- date
- amount paid into petty cash
- cheque number of cheque used to provide cash
- person/company to whom payment was made
- amount paid
- receipt number
- VAT (if you are VAT registered)
- analysis of payment (including column for 'others').

The petty cash book uses a double-entry book-keeping procedure in exactly the same way as the bank payments and deposits book.

The main difference is that you will probably need fewer analysis columns. As for payments made by cheque, you should keep all receipts, numbered individually, in a file and record the receipt numbers in your petty cash book.

VAT summary books

If you are **VAT registered** you are required to keep at least one book which acts as a summary of the VAT you have paid out, and the VAT you have charged each month. If you operate under the cash accounting scheme you could also keep a separate summary book which records every VAT payment you make each month, together with the amount of VAT received. This book isn't a requirement but will help the VAT authorities check your records.

The **cash accounting scheme** is for traders who have a gross income of less than £350,000 per year. Normally, the amount of VAT you pay to HM Customs and Excise is the difference between the amount of VAT you have *charged* in a particular quarter and the amount of VAT you have been charged. In the cash accounting scheme you only pay the difference between the amount of VAT you have actually *been* paid and the amount you have paid yourself. At first sight this may not seem important, but it is extremely helpful in improving your cash flow position.

Under the normal VAT scheme you have to pay VAT *even if you have not been paid that money by your customers.* You pay VAT according to your invoices issued each quarter. Under the cash accounting scheme you only pay what you have received, less any VAT you have paid out. This means that you do not have to pay the VAT until you receive it, thus helping your bank balance if you suffer from late payment.

VAT accounting routines
In any event you will need at least one accounts book which records the amount of VAT you have been invoiced each month, and the amount of VAT you have been charged. If you do decide to operate under the cash accounting scheme to help improve your cash flow, then you should also keep a daily summary book.

Accounting for VAT is quite simple if you have kept your bank books and petty cash books as described earlier. All you have to do each month is transfer the totals to your VAT summary book. Your VAT summary book should show:

- the net sales you have made each month
- the VAT charged each month
- the net payments made each month

INCOME

EXPENDITURE

DATE	PAID IN TO PETTY CASH	CHEQUE No	OTHER SOURCES	PAYEE	RECEIPT	AMOUNT	VAT	POSTAGE	TRAVEL	STATIONERY	OTHER ITEMS
6/2	50.00	01378		Postage	101	5.40		5.40			
8/2	25.00			Taxi Fare	102	3.20	0.48		2.72		
11/2	25.00		25.00 (Cash refund on unwanted stationey)	Postage	103	1.80		1.80			
12/2		01392		Train Fare	104	6.50			6.50		
13/2							0.48				
20/2				Stationers	105	3.20	0.48			2.72	
25/2				Print shop	106	1.24	0.18				1.06 (Photo copying)
Totals	125.00		25.00			21.34	1.14	7.20	9.22	2.72	1.06

Fig. 35. A page from a petty cash book.

VAT QUARTERLY SUMMARY
Nov 9X – Jan 9Y

		Total (Excl VAT)	VAT
Sales (Output Tax)	Nov	3000.00	525.00
	Dec	2750.00	481.25
	Jan	3250.00	568.75
		9000.00	1575.00 (A)
Purchases and expenses (Input tax)	Nov	1278.00	98.20
	Dec	1894.50	126.30
	Jan	1327.00	85.50
Petty Cash	Nov	120.10	2.50
	Dec	85.00	5.30
	Jan	90.00	3.90
		4794.60	321.70 (B)
	Balance Payable		(A-B) 1253.30

Fig. 36. A VAT quarterly summary. The purchase and expenses listed will usually include a few zero-rated or VAT-exempt purchases, so the amount of VAT recorded is not 17.5% of the total expenses figure.

- the amount of VAT you have been charged each month
- the difference between the VAT you have charged and the VAT you have paid to your suppliers. This will be the amount of VAT you pay HM Customs and Excise. If you spend more VAT than you charge you will receive a cheque for the difference from HM Customs and Excise.

If you use the cash accounting scheme, the VAT you have *received* will be used in the summary page and its calculations, instead of the VAT you have charged.

The VAT cash accounting scheme

This scheme is a benefit to virtually every home-based business that is registered for VAT. The scheme:

- is for companies with a turnover of less than £350,000 per year
- can only be used by traders approved by HM Customs and Excise
- is not available to traders who have committed any VAT offence
- helps the cash flow of small businesses by preventing them from having to pay out VAT on uncollected funds.

Preparing for annual accounts

You should keep the books up to date so that at the end of the first year of operation your accountant can prepare your **annual accounts**. If your books are badly kept, and receipts are not numbered or kept in order, your accountant will have more work to do and will charge higher fees.

You annual accounts will show the tax authorities your **turnover**, your **business expenses**, and the **profit** you have made. It is this final figure which will be used as the basis of your tax bill.

For self-employed people (the bulk of people who work from home) and for almost all small companies, tax is collected as a result of **self assessment**. Completing the self assessment forms is not easy. You will almost certainly need an accountant to help you. In addition, self assessment means you can work out your own tax. This is even more complicated. You do have the option to allow the Inland Revenue to perform the calculation for you and most accountants advise that you do this. To stay within the law and avoid automatic fines you must adhere to certain deadlines. You need to submit your tax return by 30th September each year. This gives you about four months in which to make sure your accounts are prepared. Remember this is the busiest time of the year for your accountant, so it may take time for you to get your books and records back; hence you need a set of books for each new year. Also, if you can prepare much of the work yourself, by having well-kept books and records, you will help your accountant.

Once the self assessment tax bill has been calculated by the Inland Revenue you will receive a notice of what you are due to pay. This is an **estimate** of what your tax liability for the current tax year will be (your accounts used as the basis of assessment are from the previous tax year). The amount the Inland Revenue estimates is due in two instalments payable by 31st January and 31st July. Automatic fines and interest payments apply if you fail to pay up. If the amount estimated is too high, you will receive a refund from the Inland Revenue, usually in August, after you have made the second payment. If the amount estimated proves to be too low (since the Inland Revenue now has the benefit of seeing what you actually earned, as your following year's accounts have been submitted by this time) you will owe the extra tax and will be sent a bill payable immediately.

Be sure to put the estimated amount aside, in a deposit account of some kind. If you don't do this you will have problems when the bill is due to be paid. Tax bills must be paid on time! Remember:

● The Inland Revenue has penalties for late payment of taxes.
● Withholding information on your financial affairs from the Inland Revenue can be construed as fraud which can be punished by imprisonment.

Inspections
The **Inland Revenue** and **HM Customs and Excise** both have the right to demand inspection of your business premises and all your accounts. Inspections can be held at a moment's notice, and you should therefore have your accounts up to date. Telling the local tax inspector you are sorry that your book-keeping is three months behind will not suffice. Be sure to keep your books every week, if not every day.

A tax inspector will need to see the following records in his inspection:

● all your accounting books
● bank statements
● building society pass books/statements
● cheque stubs
● copies of invoices
● loan statements/agreements
● personal financial information (such as personal account bank statements, mortgage statements, etc)

- receipts for petty cash payments
- receipts from cheque payments
- VAT returns (if registered)
- any other financial information, including joint accounts with your wife/husband.

Your must keep all of these records for a minimum period of six years to satisfy the financial authorities.

Accounting with computers

If you use a computer in your business it could help in running your accounts, but the program you buy should be able to satisfy the requirements of:

- your accountant
- the local tax inspector
- inspectors from HM Customs and Excise.

It would be best to ask for advice from these people before committing yourself. The program should be able to perform proper double-entry book-keeping procedures, and enable you to identify a payment, its date, and analysis, simply, for example, from a receipt number or a cheque number. In other words, it must be capable of a great deal of flexibility and sophistication, which generally means that you will need to spend a lot of money on it. Cheap programs are available, but their facilities are usually limited and are unlikely to satisfy the financial authorities.

If you do decide to computerise your accounts it is wise to keep manual records for the first year so that your accountant, and the tax authorities, can make any checks they want on the system you are using, and also keep a printout of your computerised accounts, just in case the machine goes wrong!

MANAGEMENT INFORMATION

Your annual accounts, and even your book-keeping procedures, will provide a great deal of management information. You will be able, for example, to work out the percentage profit you have made on your sales; you will be able to spot any areas in which you are spending too much money, thus enabling you to cut back in the following year. You will also be able to see how much you are worth! Your annual accounts will include information on your **current assets**.

Current assets

Your current assets include all the money you have in the bank or building society plus the value of the equipment and raw materials you have bought, plus the value of any money you are owed. Essentially, this figure shows what you own should the worst happen and you have to sell everything associated with the business, and pay off your debts

The current assets figure is essential in helping you to determine your ability to continue running the business. It helps you to calculate a very important 'financial ratio'. These ratios help financiers assess your business to a reasonable degree of accuracy. The most important ratio is the following:

$$\frac{\text{Current Assets}}{\text{Current Liabilities}}$$

In other words, divide the current assets figure in your annual accounts by the amount of money you owe to show whether you would be able to pay off all your debts and still have money in your pocket should you stop trading. If this calculation results in a final figure of two or more you are on the road to success. If the ratio is just one, you would be able to pay your debts but would be penniless afterwards. Naturally, a figure of less than one means that you could be in trouble if you ceased trading, as you could not pay your debts! If you become insolvent you should cease running up new debts.

Reducing late payers

One thing which can badly affect your cash flow, is the late payment of invoices. Some people seem to take an inordinate amount of time to settle their accounts with small businesses. Late payments will be highlighted in your sales book, and should not be tolerated. One of the main reasons for the failure of small businesses is late payment.

In order to reduce this problem, adopt the following steps:

- Write 'Payment due within 30 days' on all invoices.
- Point out on all quotations that you do not give extended credit.
- Telephone customers if you have not received payment on the 31st day after the date of the invoice and tell them that payment is late.

In many instances these measures will resolve the problem. However, some customers, *particularly large businesses*, will hold off payment to a small business for as long as possible. This is totally unacceptable. If you quote your terms in your invoice your customer is in breach of contract if payment is not received by you in that time. You can therefore legitimately threaten legal action. Indeed, if you establish a good relationship with a local solicitor you will be able to get him or her to send out a letter to this effect. It costs around £10 a time, and almost always achieves instant results. If the amount you are owed is less than £1000 you can use the arbitration procedure of the Small Claims Division of the County Court. All court fees are paid by your customer and not by you. You can also use this scheme without a solicitor, although you ought to obtain legal advice in each case to ensure that this is the most appropriate procedure for your needs. The Small Claims procedure can also be used for larger amounts, but is more complicated and would need the help of a solicitor.

Whatever kind of home-based business you operate, remember:

● Late payers reduce your monthly income and consequently lower the amount of cash you have available to run your business. Don't let such people ruin your business.

TAKING OUT INSURANCE

Far too many people ignore insurance. The self-employed do so at their peril. What if your home burns down, destroying your business records and equipment? What if you fall ill and are unable to work for two months? What if you have an accident and are unable to perform the same work-related tasks as before? Anyone who runs a business from home should seriously consider the following forms of insurance:

● accident insurance
● equipment insurance
● life assurance and pension
● permanent health insurance
● professional indemnity insurance.

Accident insurance

A small premium of around £25 per month will cover you for the loss of limbs, fingers, eyes, etc, as a result of an accident. This sort of policy would pay out around £50,000 if you lost a limb, or £10,000 if you lost the hearing in one ear. Such incidents could seriously affect your ability to earn money in a home-based business and therefore the cover would provide you with cash to cover any changes necessary for you to carry on working.

Equipment insurance

If you use any equipment in your work you should insure it against theft or damage by fire. Your work will be drastically hampered if such equipment is removed or destroyed, and the premiums are not high. Something like £10,000 worth of equipment will cost only around £250 per year to insure against such risks. You will not usually be able to insure all your business equipment under your household insurance if you work from home. Materials used for business purposes are generally excluded from such policies so you will need to insure all your business items separately.

Life assurance and pension

Your most valuable asset is yourself. At death, we leave behind all our debts, plus the care of any dependents in the future. If you do not plan for such provisions you will leave nothing but financial mess in your wake. The most cost-effective way of providing life assurance, especially if you are self-employed, is to take out a pension-linked policy.

Under normal circumstances, life assurance is not a tax-deductible expense. However, pension premiums *are* tax-deductible, and linking life assurance to such policies is extremely cheap. You therefore gain the benefit of a low-cost method of life assurance plus the benefit of tax relief.

Anyone who runs their own business should have a pension plan. The pension you will receive from the state is minimal. For advice on the best sort of plan for you, contact your bank manager and your accountant who will be able to put you in touch with the relevant consultants for advice. You should aim to spend around 8% of your profits on pension premiums each year. Adding life assurance to these premiums could cost a mere £60 per year and will provide a high level of cover. For example, if you pay £125 per month on pension and life assurance, only around £5 of this will be the life assurance premium yet you could be covered for around £140,000. You could not achieve such cost-effective cover by buying life assurance alone.

There are other forms of life assurance and the best policy will depend upon your age, health and other personal circumstances. Get a good broker to recommend the policy most suitable (see page 148). Brokers can also deal with your pension requirements.

Your bank manager will also be able to offer some advice on pensions and life assurance. However, it is worth noting that the banks were required in 1988 to decide whether they would offer totally independent advice on pensions and insurance or simply offer one set of 'products'. Most now offer their own products rather than being independent.

Permanent health insurance

If you are ill when you are working for yourself, and are unable to work, you will not get paid. By taking out Permanent Health Insurance (PHI) you will be able to cover yourself for such eventualities. A premium of around £125 per month could pay out around £1,800 per month if you became ill and could not work as a result.

Professional indemnity insurance

You may need to cover yourself against claims for faulty manufacture, or maladministration. Professional indemnity insurance would provide cover for such problems. Few insurance companies offer such policies, and you may need a broker to help you. Two of the best-known firms providing these policies are Royal Sun Alliance and Norwich Union. Premiums will depend on the level of cover you want and the level and nature of your business.

Getting insurance

Getting insurance is easiest through a broker. Your accountant or bank manager will be able to recommend good brokers. Alternatively you could contact the British Insurance & Investment Brokers Association for a list of members in your area. (Fountain House, 14 Bevis Marks, London EC3A 7NT. Tel: 020 7623 9043). For further advice on all business insurance matters contact the Association of British Insurers (ABI), 51 Gresham Street, London EC2V 7HQ. Tel: 020 7600 3333.

CHECKLIST

● Always keep up-to-date and accurate accounts.
● Invoice customers as soon as work is completed, stating terms.
● Always press customers to pay on time.
● Use your annual accounts to measure your performance and to alter any areas which are overspent.
● Insure your business activities against possible damage as a result of physical or personal loss.

10

Staying in Business

ENTHUSIASM AND COMMON SENSE

Having got your home-based business started, you will be full of enthusiasm, looking forward to increasing your earnings, and thoroughly
enjoying the freedom of self-employment. That is what self-employment
is all about. But while you are enjoying the pleasures of your new life, it
is as well to be aware of, and guard against, problems which could cause
your enthusiasm to wane.

Check your commitment to the business

Once you have started, answer the following questions to see whether
you are losing any enthusiasm for your business and to help you analyse
whether you are performing well.

1. How many hours per week do you now work?   _____

2. How many hours do you spend on administration?   _____

3. What is the ratio of time you spend on
    administration compared to total work hours?   _____

4. Do you find that you start work later than
    when the business was beginning?   _____

5. Do you find that you finish work earlier?   _____

6. Do you take days off each week?   _____

7. Do you find it hard to concentrate?   _____

8. Do you nip out of your workplace to
    watch television programmes during the day?   _____

9. Do you visit a local pub most lunchtimes?   _____

10. Do you actually feel less inclined to
    work now than when you started the business?   _____

If you answer 'Yes' to the last seven questions your business is in danger. You have lost that initial burst of enthusiasm and you need to take action to keep yourself in business and restore some enthusiasm.

Administration

Many businesses fail because the initial enthusiasm begins to wane as the owner becomes fed up with administration, book-keeping and filing, but your business will not survive for long if you do not attend to such administrative duties. You may, for example, absolutely adore making cuddly toys for sale in local shops, but if you spend all your time making the toys, and ignoring the administration, your business will eventually collapse.

You probably started your own business because it involved doing a job which you enjoyed. Very few people start businesses because they love the administration! But administration is vital to the proper running of any business. If you neglect it your business will not perform properly and will slowly but surely die. You should budget your time to allow for the following golden rule:

● **Administration is vital and must never be overlooked**.

If you are aware from the start of the need for administration, and allow time for it, it will become less of a burden.

Time management

Time management is not a new 'yuppie' concept. It has been around for many years. Schools, for example, have carefully planned and managed timetables and so have many organisations. By timetabling your day-to-day activities you can become much more efficient than if you simply start each day with a pile of work and attempt to sort your way through it.

You can buy pre-packed time management systems, like a Filofax, from most stationers and department stores, and every home-based business should have a time management system of some kind. You do not necessarily have to buy the pre-packed systems, and you can produce your own, but it is worthwhile getting something like a Filofax if you are new to the concept of time management.

You can also now get time management programs for your computer. These can automatically forward missed tasks and make sure appointments don't overlap. One of the most comprehensive and easy-to-use programs is Microsoft Outlook. This is provided as part of the Microsoft Office package of software. However, you can also buy Outlook as a stand alone program if you wish. It is also available on the internet from www.microsoft.com.

When using a time management system you set yourself targets which you know you can reach, and then prepare a timetable which will allow you to achieve what you want. On each page of a time manager you will have time slots in which you write the work you must complete each day, as well as any specific tasks that need doing such as telephone calls.

Use a time manager to slot in your administrative duties — many people find it easier to allow the first hour or two of each day to get the administration out of the way, before getting on with the 'proper' work. In this way you will keep up-to-date with the administration. Indeed, seeing piles of administrative work waiting to be done is one of the things which puts you off working. If you can keep it under control by planning your time effectively you will not lose your enthusiasm so easily. To get the most from your time manager, use the following procedure:

- Set aside 15 minutes at the end of each day to plan your next day's work.
- Write in your time manager everything you must do. If you do not complete these jobs on one particular day write them down for another day.
- Write down the names of people you must contact each day.
- Tick off each task once you have completed it.
- Open up your time manager at the beginning of the day and look at what has to be done.
- Always carry your time manager with you.

Keeping financial control

Many businesses fail to succeed because of poor financial control. The last chapter showed you how to keep your accounts accurately, and how to deal with the various financial authorities. However, simply keeping good accounts is not enough to maintain control over your finances. You must:

- review your spending every month and cut back in overspent areas
- review your customer base each month and construct new marketing plans if custom is insufficient
- analyse your accounts every quarter and calculate the ratio of current assets to current liabilities
- reconcile your bank statements each month (ie verify which cheques

have been presented and that everything has been passed through your bank account accurately)
- follow cost-saving procedures such as using the telephone only during the cheaper rate periods
- review your annual accounts and discuss ways of saving with your accountant.

You should also provide time slots in your time management system for book-keeping so that you keep up-to-date with your books. By providing an hour each week in your time manager you will be able to keep a close eye on your finances. If you only do your books every two or three months you will be working in the financial dark, and could lose money.

Using contacts

Another reason for the loss of initial business enthusiasm is loneliness. People who run home-based businesses generally work alone and you need considerable drive and ambition to overcome feelings of loneliness and isolation.

Moreover, because you are alone there is often no one to turn to for friendly advice, or to bounce ideas off. This can worry some self-employed people. It often helps to talk to other people in your situation — people who work at home. You can do this by joining the local Chamber of Commerce, which will have many small business members. Also, you may find local support organisations by contacting your local Business Link. In addition you can find out more about other home based businesses from the monthly newsletter *Better Business*. This costs £72 per year and is available from the publishers at: Active Information, Cribau Mill, Llanvair Discoed, Chepstow NP6 6RD or email: info@better-business.co.uk.

Managing stress

Stress is a very real problem for people who run their own home-based business. You will worry that you may not succeed, that you may not have enough customers, or that you may not be able to cope with the financial pressures. Such worries inevitably lead to stress, and that could affect your health. If you suffer from stress, and your health fails as a result, your business activities will suffer, so to keep in business you must manage stress properly. To help avoid excessive stress you should:

- manage your time effectively — make time (at least 15 minutes every day) to plan your day

- make sure you have adequate breaks during the day — at least 30 minutes for lunch, and two other breaks of at least 15 minutes
- lie down and relax for 20 minutes at the end of each day without interruption
- avoid excessive amounts of alcohol
- eat a well-balanced healthy diet
- get plenty of exercise.

If you can manage stress in your working life you will be able to help yourself keep in business.

Managing legal problems

Another area which could present problems once your business is up and running is the law. If you become involved in legal disputes you could damage your business beyond repair so be sure that your business is operating legally. Apart from laws relating to the use of your home for business purposes, mentioned in Chapter 2, there are other laws which might affect you. These include the following:

- Companies Act
- Consumer Protection Acts
- Copyright Acts
- Employment legislation
- Fair Trading Act
- Health and Safety at Work Act
- Industrial Relations Act
- Insolvency Act
- Law of contract
- Partnership Act
- Patents
- Sale of Goods Act
- Trade Descriptions Acts.

As you can see, there is a plethora of legislation which could affect your business. The best way to avoid subsequent legal problems is to seek legal advice when setting up your business.

Contracts

The legislation relating to contracts is one area of law which is likely to affect all home-based businesses. Customers can sue you for **damages** (compensation) if you fail to meet the agreed terms of a business contract. If you do not supply materials on time you will be in breach of contract, as you would be if you failed to pay your bills on time. To avoid contractual problems draw up a simple agreement for your business (get your solicitor to help you) and use this as your **Terms of Trading**. Give a copy to every customer for acceptance before settling any deal so that you can avoid arguments, and potential legal problems.

TROUBLESHOOTING

It's a daunting fact that only about five of every 100 new businesses survive for more than five years — and the vast majority of those 95 failures take place in the first twelve months of trading. So how can you make sure of being one of the five, and not one of the 95? One important aspect is **troubleshooting** — anticipating the potential problems your business will have and tackling them head on.

Troubleshooting should become a routine. Apart from predicting troubles when your business is starting, you should make time specifically for tackling problems at least once every three months. This troubleshooting routine should systematically deal with at least the following three areas:

● assessing business plans, including updating if necessary
● identifying potential financial worries
● dealing with domestic difficulties.

Mark down one date at least every three months for this — and allow at least half that day, if not all of it, for troubleshooting. On the day, make sure you have all the information you need on your desk. You will need your accounts books, original business plan and so on, together with any extra data on your current situation such as your order book and a list of potential new clients.

Using this information, draw up your new cash flow forecasts, marketing plans and so on. Having done this, write down a list of suggestions to yourself to improve your business over the next three months. Keep this list of action points pinned to your wall above your desk so that you know every day over the next three months what must be done to improve your business. Such permanent reminders of tasks you must perform will help considerably in your attempts to stay in business. If you go through this routine each quarter but then don't act on your conclusions, you'll be wasting your time. So your action plan should be:

● Set aside a day each quarter for troubleshooting.

- Have any necessary information to hand.

- Review the progress of your business, dealing with any problems which have arisen since your last troubleshooting session.

- Write a plan of action for avoiding these problems in the future.

- Pin the plan above your workspace.

- **Act on it!**

Now let's look at the three major trouble shooting areas in more detail.

Updating your business plan

The plans and forecasts you make when starting will have to be adapted to the changing needs of your business and your customers. It is therefore essential that you replan your business periodically to make sure you stay on the right track.

Your overall business plan will be a document which outlines your strategy for the next three years. Rewrite the plan each year, altering the cash flow predictions and changing your marketing strategy to suit the way your business develops. This will mean reviewing your business plan every three months — perhaps as part of your troubleshooting exercise to make sure you stay on course. Try the following routine.

- Reread your business plan.

- Note down changes in circumstances.

- Recalculate your cash flow predictions.

- Replan your marketing strategies.

Next write a short, quarterly **plan of campaign** together with your financial assessment in the form of a cash flow forecast for the remainder of the year. At the end of the year, use your quarterly re-appraisals to prepare your business plan for the coming three years. Thus you can produce **rolling** business plans so that you know exactly how you intend to operate for the next three years.

If you only produce one three year business plan at the start of your business you will be operating in the dark during your fourth year. Your business will only succeed if you constantly update your business plans and cash flow forecasts.

TERMS OF TRADING

1. The Petcare Hotel agrees to provide accommodation and food for animals entrusted to its care.

2. All accommodation is in a centrally heated area.

3. Food supplied is standard animal feedstuff. Any special dietary requirements must be notified to the Petcare Hotel in advance. Special diets will require additional payments above the standard charges.

4. No animals with signs of infectious diseases will be admitted to the Petcare Hotel. The Petcare Hotel will seek veterinary advice in cases of doubt. Owners must not seek accommodation for their pets if they know of any infectious illnesses from which the animal suffers.

5. Veterinary attention will be provided should any pet become ill during its stay at The Petcare Hotel. The fees for such attention will be added to the final invoice.

6. The Petcare Hotel will not be responsible for any diseases pets contract as a result of the negligence of other owners who ignore Clause 4.

7. All fees are payable within 30 days of admission of the pet to The Petcare Hotel. An invoice will be issued upon delivery of the animal to the Hotel. Any additional fees will be presented on a final invoice issued at the time of collection of the animal.

Fig. 37. The terms of trading which the Petcare Hotel might be able to offer.

Financial troubleshooting

To keep an eye on your finances, begin by analysing the income you receive each quarter and comparing this with your expenditure. This will be easy if your accounts are kept up to date and your bank statements are properly reconciled. You can immediately see whether you are in the red or in the black.

Your current ratio

Next, calculate your **current ratio** (see Chapter 9) to find out if you could afford to pay all your debts in your current financial state. If you *can* do this and have some cash to spare your business is doing reasonably well. If your current liabilities are greater than your current assets you are in trouble.

Ideally, your current ratio should be two or higher, which means you have twice as much money as you need to pay off your debts. Check your current ratio each quarter as part of your financial troubleshooting exercise. If it is less than two, try to improve the situation — ideally by getting more cash paid into your business.

Don't forget that buyers of your products or services who delay payment are reducing your current assets. Although your accountant will include such owed money as 'debtors' in your end of year accounts and include this figure in your current assets calculation, this is merely a paper exercise. For your financial troubleshooting it is wise to restrict current assets to **stock** and **cash in hand**. It's no use saying to all the people to whom you owe money that you don't have any at the moment since your customers haven't paid up! Your true day-to-day current asset status is best seen in terms of actual cash available.

Controlling credit

So if your current asset figure begins to fall, tighten up control of the amount of credit terms from 30 days to only 14 days, for example, or to chase certain customers. Some of your customers will repeatedly fail to meet your deadlines and may not respond to your requests for payment. Give notice to such customers that you will do no more work for them if they do not pay up their existing debts and that you will substantially reduce the credit terms you give them in future.

Ideally, you should give your customers a **credit limit**. This is the maximum amount of unpaid invoices they are allowed to accumulate before you stop working for them. Your quarterly troubleshooting sessions will be able to check whether each customer has gone above their credit limit. Your troubleshooting session will also enable you to review the individual credit limits you have applied and to adjust them according to the value of the business each customer provides.

But remember — there are two sides to the coin. Reducing your credit limit might put customers off using you altogether. Ultimately, it depends on the nature of your business, and the financial standing of your customers.

You may find that you have the 'credit limit' problem in reverse: how soon should you pay your *own* bills? Do you need to negotiate for better credit terms from your suppliers? This will depend on your situation. Most people starting up should try to keep their overheads to a minimum — negotiate the best credit terms possible for your first deals. However, as your business begins to grow, you may find that prompt payment or even payment in cash can have its own advantages — often suppliers will offer better terms, and your bargaining position will be stronger if you have the money in your hand. It's your decision.

There is one important rule, however: *Pay your bills on time*. There is no advantage in establishing a reputation as a 'poor risk' — people will merely be more reluctant to provide the service you need at the price you want.

Checking profitability
The final part of your financial troubleshooting routine should analyse your **profits**. Concentrating on your current ratio will determine the overall stability of your business, but it is your profit figure which will show whether your business is really booming or not. Your profits will be the difference between your income and your expenditure. Check this difference each quarter. Ideally it should grow over the year. Are your profits climbing or falling? Take action to reduce expenditure or increase income if your profits stagnate or fall. The action you need to take should be included in your rewritten business plan each quarter and reassessed every three months as part of your trouble-shooting routine.

Personnel troubleshooting
Problems with your family or with anyone who helps you out can prove fatal for your business and must be avoided at all costs. This area is often underestimated as a cause of business failure. A perfect cash flow forecast and a brilliant strategy will not work if the people involved in the business cannot co-operate. Most home-based businesses only involve one person, but there are other potential personnel problems which can damage the business irreparably.

Your business plan should have pinpointed any family squabbles which could occur. These must be sorted out before you start the business — but reappraise the situation every three months to check that matters have been adequately dealt with. Also, as your business grows and develops, new problems will surface and these must be faced and sorted out if the business is not to suffer. Any changes in family or domestic circumstances will need considering and you may need to adapt the way you work to cope with the new situation.

Some of the changes which can affect your home-based business are:

● marriage
● children
● divorce
● death of a loved one
● relocation due to partner's job
● change in partner's job
● new neighbours.

All of these may lead to 'people problems' at work. A change in your partner's job may mean that your working day is disrupted if he or she starts coming home earlier than in the past, or new neighbours may have children who play in the garden beneath your office window and make it harder for you to concentrate. You may need to adapt your own routine to those around you — and the fact that you *can* is one of the great advantages of working from home. For example, if your partners *does* start coming home earlier and disrupts your day you have plenty of options:

● start work earlier
● work Saturday mornings
● reduce your lunch break
● cut your income and cut your expenses.

Luckily for you, the choice is yours.

THE SECRET OF STAYING IN BUSINESS

There are plenty of people who will tell you they know of a sure way of making it in business, and each one has a different theory. In fact, there is not really a magic formula which will make you a millionaire overnight. There is, however, one rule which every business should always have in mind — the simple golden rule without which you will almost certainly fail:

● **Provide your customers with the right product, at the right time, and at the right price**.

Hopefully, this book will have also given you some idea of the importance of planning when setting up a business. As a general rule of thumb, you can never spend too much time on planning, no matter how well-prepared you think you may be. Having read this book, you should know roughly what starting a business from home entails. The rest is up to you. Good luck!

CHECKLIST

● Guard against loss of enthusiasm.
● Keep up with administrative tasks so that they do not become a major burden.
● Keep a time management system so that you can manage your time effectively.
● Keep a close watch on your finances.
● Get in touch with other home-based workers to overcome loneliness.
● Take steps to avoid stress.
● Take legal advice to avoid damaging legal problems.
● Perform regular troubleshooting reviews and adapt your work accordingly.

Glossary

Access provider A company that provides you with the necessary software and codes for getting on the internet.

Accident insurance Insurance which covers people for loss of use of parts of their body following an accident.

Accountancy The production of legal documents outlining the financial aspects of a business operation.

Advertising Promotion of a business by messages in the media.

Assets The total value of things owned by a business.

Book-keeping The production of records of a business's financial transactions.

Business plan A written guide to the aims of a business with details of how those aims will be achieved.

Cash book The accounting book which records all payments into and out of the business's bank account.

Cash flow forecast A detailed and well-researched estimate of the money coming into and going out from a business.

Change of use certificate A document provided by planning authorities when planning permission is granted for buildings to be used for different purposes from those for which they were built.

Customer service The added extras which businesses provide to ensure continued customer satisfaction, thus achieving loyalty amongst the purchasers of products and services.

Direct mail Advertising and promotional material delivered to a specific and carefully targeted audience.

Fees The charges which a business makes for services and products.

Financial control The careful assessment of how much a business is receiving and how much it is spending, in order to ensure that cash is spent wisely, and that marketing campaigns are working.

Internet Service Provider (ISP) *see* Access Provider.

Liabilities The money which a business owes in the forms of loans, hire purchase agreements, trade suppliers, tax etc.

Life assurance A form of insurance which pays an agreed sum in the event of the death of the insured person.

Limited company A separate legal entity which can trade in its own right. Forming limited companies can have tax advantages, and can protect the owners from paying debts if the firm runs into trouble.

Loss The difference which results when a business spends more than it earns.

Marketing plan A written document which details the financial objectives of a business and explains how a range of advertising and public relations activities will achieve those aims.

National Insurance The charges made by the Government to cover services such as the National Health Service and the state pension scheme.

Partnership A legally binding agreement between two or more individuals to trade together as one.

Pension A scheme, usually operated by insurance companies, which provides income on retirement.

Permanent Health Insurance An insurance scheme which covers the individual for loss of income owing to illness.

Planning permission The legal permission which is granted by local authorities for individuals or businesses to build or change the use of premises. Planning permission may be necessary for some home-based businesses.

Professional indemnity An insurance scheme which protects businesses against claims for problems involved in the running of the business, such as administrative errors.

Profit The difference which results when a business earns more than it spends.

Public relations The use of the press and other institutions such as exhibitions and conferences, to help promote a business.

Purchase book The accounting book which records details of money which a business spends on purchases.

Sales book The accounting book which records details of money which comes into a business as a result of its trading.

Sole trader A self-employed individual.

Tax Money paid to the Government as a result of financial activities. Most people who run a business from home are taxed on their profits.

Tax relief Money which can be claimed as expenses required to run a business, thus reducing profit, and thereby cutting down the level of tax which has to be paid.

Time management The timetabling of business and personal life so as to enjoy maximum efficiency.

Training & Enterprise Councils (TECs) A nationwide network of bodies set up to foster skills training and business enterprise.

Operating under broad government guidelines, each regional TEC is a partnership of local public organisations and businesses, and devises its own programmes of financial support and advice. See your local phone book for details.

Turnover The total amount of money which comes into a business from all sources.

VAT Value Added Tax. A tax applied to a wide range of products and services.

Further Reading

BOOKS

101 Great Money Making Ideas, Mark Hempshell (Northcote House)

Business Ripoffs and How to Avoid Them, Tony Attwood (Kogan Page)

Doing Business on the Internet, Graham Jones, (How to Books, 1997)

Finance for Small Business, Keith Checkley (Sphere Reference, 1984)

How to Do Your Own Advertising, Michael Bennie (Northcote House)

How to Manage Computers at Work, Graham Jones (How To Books, 1993)

How to Publish a Newsletter, Graham Jones (How To Books, 1992)

How to Raise Business Finance, Peter Ibbetson (Northcote House)

How to Sell a Service, Malcolm McDonald and John Leppart (Heinemann, 1986)

How to Win Customers, Heinz Goldmann (Pan, London, 1980)

How to Work from Home, Ian Phillipson (How To Books, 2nd edition, 1995)

Law for the Small Business, Patricia Clayton (Kogan Page, 1987)

Managing Budgets & Cash Flows, Peter Taylor (How To Books, 2nd edition, 1996)

Mastering Business English, Michael Bennie (How To Books, 4th edition 1998)

Managing your Business Accounts, Peter Taylor (How To Books, 4th edition 1998)

Money for Business (Bank of England)

Notes to Help You (Data Protection Registrar, Wilmslow, Cheshire)

Small Business Handbook (Lloyds Bank)

Small Business Insurance Advice File (Association of British Insurers)

Sources of Free Business Information, Michael Brooks (Kogan Page, 1986)

Successful Marketing for the Small Business, Dave Patten (Kogan Page)

Support for Business (Department of Trade and Industry)

Tax for the Self-Employed, Richard Edwards (Oyez Longman)

Time for Success, James Noon (International Thomson Publishing, London, 1983)

The VAT Guide (HM Customs and Excise)

Using the Internet, Graham Jones (How to Books, 1999)
Why you need a Chartered Accountant (Institute of Chartered Accountants)
Writing a Press Release, Peter Bartram (How To Books, 3rd edition, 1999)
Your Business and the Law, John Harris (Oyez Longman, London)

For a list of business books go to www.amazon.co.uk on the internet.

PERIODICALS

Better Business: the business on giving you the business edge. Active Information, Criban Mill, Llanvair Discoed, Chepstow NP6 6RD. Tel: (01291) 641222.

Useful Addresses

A short book of this kind can only be a guide to the way to set up a home-based business. You will no doubt need further information and advice on starting your business, running it, and expanding in the future. To help you find that information and advice, here is a comprehensive list of contacts which may be of help.

FINANCIAL

Association of British Insurers, 51 Gresham Street, London EC2V 7 HQ. Tel: 020 7600 3333.

Bank of England, London EC2R 8AH. Tel: 020 7601 4444.

Bank of Scotland, The Mound, Edinburgh EH1 1YZ. Tel: (0131) 243 5441.

Barclays Bank PLC, 54 Lombard Street, London EC3N 3HJ. Tel: 020 7699 5000.

British Insurance & Investment Brokers Association, BIBA House, 14 Bevis Marks, London EC3A 7NT. Tel: 020 7623 9043.

Chartered Association of Certified Accountants, 29 Lincoln's Inn Fields, London WC2. Tel: 020 7242 6855.

Clydesdale Bank PLC, 150 Buchanan Street, Glasgow G1 2HL. Tel: (0141) 223 2853.

Co-operative Bank PLC, PO Box 101, 1 Balloon Street, Manchester M60 4EP. Tel: (0161) 832 3456.

Department of Social Security, 79 Whitehall, London SW1A 2NS. (For local office see 'contributions agency' in the Phone Book).

Girobank PLC, 49 Park Lane, London W1Y 4EQ. Tel: 020 7396 6464.

HM Customs and Excise, New King's Beam House, 22 Upper Ground, London SE1 9PJ. Tel: 020 7620 1313.

HSBC PLC, 27 Poultry, London EC2P 2BX. Tel: 020 7260 8000.

Inland Revenue, Bush House, The Strand, London WC2B 4PP. Tel: 020 7438 6692.

Institute of Chartered Accountants of England and Wales, PO Box 433, Chartered Accountants Hall, Moorgate Place, London EC2P 2BJ. Tel: 020 7920 8100.

Institute of Chartered Accountants of Scotland, 27 Queen Street, Edinburgh EH2 1LA.

Lloyds TSB PLC, PO Box 215, 71 Lombard Street, London EC3P 3BS. Tel: 020 7626 1500.

National Savings, Charles House, 375 Kensington High Street, London W14. Tel: 020 7605 9300.

National Westminster Bank PLC, 41 Lothbury, London EC2P 2BP. Tel: 020 7726 1000.

Royal Bank of Scotland, PO Box 31, 42 St Andrew Square, Edinburgh EH2 2YE. Tel: (0131) 556 8555.

MARKETING

Advertising Association, Abford House, 15 Wilton Road, London SW1. Tel: 020 7828 2771.

Advertising Standards Authority, 2 Torrington Place, London WC1. Tel: 020 7580 5555.

British Direct Marketing Association, Haymarket House, 1 Oxendon St, London SW1Y 4EE. Tel: 020 7321 2525.

Institute of Practitioners in Advertising, 44 Belgrave Square, London SW1X 8QS. Tel: 020 7235 7020.

Institute of Public Relations, 15 Northburgh Street, London EC1V 0PR Tel: 020 7253 5151.

Institute of Sales Promotion, 66 Pentonville Road, London N1 9HS. Tel: 020 7837 5340.

MANAGEMENT

British Chambers of Commerce, 9 Tufton Street, London SW1P 3QB. Tel: 020 7222 1555.

Central Office of Information, Hercules Road, London SE1 7DU. Tel: 020 7928 2345.

Commission for Racial Equality, Elliot House, 10 Allington Street, London SW1 5EH. Tel: 020 7828 7022.

Companies House, Crown Way, Maindy, Cardiff CF4 3UZ.

Companies Registration Office (Scotland), 102 George Street, Edinburgh EH2 3DJ.

Confederation of British Industry, Centre Point, 103 New Oxford Street, London WC1A 1DU. Tel: 020 7395 8239.

Consumers' Association, 2 Marylebone Road, London NW1 4DF. Tel: 020 7830 6000.

Data Protection Registrar, Wycliffe House, Water Lane, Wilmslow, Cheshire SK9 5AF. Tel: (01625) 545745.

Department of the Environment, 2 Marsham Street, London SW1P 3EB. Tel: 020 7276 0900.

Department of Trade and Industry, 1 Victoria Street, London SW1E 6RB. Tel: 020 7215 5000.

Equal Opportunities Commission, Overseas House, Quay Street, Manchester M3 3HN. Tel: (0161) 833 9244.

Federation of Small Business, 2 Catherine Place, London SW1E 6HF. Tel: 020 7233 7900.

Institute of Management, 2 Savoy Court, The Strand, London WC2R 0EZ. Tel: 020 7497 0580.

LEGAL MATTERS

Law Society, 113 Chancery Lane, London WC2. Tel: 020 7242 1222.

Office of Fair Trading, Field House, Breams Buildings, London EC4A 1PR. Tel: 020 7211 8000.

Royal Town Planning Institute, 26 Portland Place, London W1N 4BE. Tel: 020 7636 9107.

Index

BECOMING A CONSULTANT
How to start and run a profitable consulting business

Susan Nash

Consulting has become a lucrative and growing working option. This book will provide you with the methodology to set up and run your own consulting business and an understanding of the steps you need to take to make it successful. It will enable you to define your business's strategic direction and give you the practical skills to make your business a reality. You will learn how to raise finances, maintain financial control, implement a marketing strategy and deliver on-going business. Susan Nash is the British President of EM-Power, a US based consulting firm which has worked with over 50 companies in both the UK and USA. She has presented the workshop 'Consulting and Making Money At It', for the past seven years.

144pp. illus. 1 85703 392 2.

STARTING YOUR OWN BUSINESS
How to plan and create a successful enterprise

Jim Green

Now in its second edition, this dynamic guide fully explores the vital steps to creating a business. It will show you how to galvanise into action, how to write a winning plan, how to approach potential funders, how to present a case for public sector assistance, how to market your business and how to develop the selling habit. 'Practical advice presented in a clear and concise style.' *Moneywise.*

159pp. illus. 1 85703 274 8. 2nd edition.

WRITING A PRESS RELEASE
How to get the right kind of publicity and news coverage

Peter Bartram

Which stories make an editor sit up and take notice? Why do some press releases never get used? This book explains all. 'Takes you step-by-step through the process.' *Home Run Magazine.* 'Shows you how to style and build a news story that carries value for readers . . . I recommend this book.' *Writers Forum.* 'Yes! Here at last is a book that tells it like it is.' Phoenix, Association of Graduate Careers Advisory Services.

144pp. illus. 1 85703 485 6. 3rd edition.

GETTING MORE BUSINESS
How to gain new customers using proven marketing techniques

Sallyann Sheridan

People and companies who get ahead don't always have the greatest product or service – they simply use the best marketing techniques. This exciting new book explains those proven techniques, using case studies and examples throughout. Discover how to create and write effective sales letters and how to get the best deals for your advertising. Learn how to sell to your customers again and again, and then get them working for you! If you have a product or service to sell, this book is for you. It will save you time and money, and help your business grow. As a professional marketing writer, Sallyann Sheridan works with a wide range of companies, products and services, many of them world leaders.

144 pp. illus. 1 85703 480 5.

MAKING DIRECT MAIL WORK
How to boost your profits with effective direct mail promotion

Peter Arnold

Direct mail is a proven and effective method of promotion for almost every type of organisation, large or small. Love it or hate it, direct mail works. Any small company, or even self-employed people, can take advantage of this most flexible and controllable of all promotional media. This book sets out, in a simple and graphic way, exactly how to initiate and run your own direct mail system. It also shows you how to avoid the pitfalls and maximise effectiveness and efficiency. Peter Arnold has been creating and writing direct mail campaigns for over 35 years, and is one of the most experienced professionals in Britain. He has worked for every sort of organisation from the large multinational to the one and two-man operation.

144pp. illus. 1 85703 297 7.

MANAGING YOUR PERSONAL FINANCES
How to achieve your own financial security, wealth and independence

John Claxton

Life for most people has become increasingly troubled by financial worries, both at home and at work, whilst the once dependable welfare state is shrinking. This book, now revised and updated, will help you to prepare a strategy towards creating your own financial independence. Find out in simple language: how to avoid debt, how to prepare for possible incapacity or redundancy, and how to finance your retirement, including care in old age. Discover how to acquire new financial skills, increase your income, reduce outgoings, and prepare to survive in a more self-reliant world. John Claxton is a Chartered Management Accountant and Chartered Secretary. He teaches personal money management in adult education.

160pp. illus. 1 85703 471 6. 3rd edition.